THE CHRISTIAN'S STRATEGIES FOR

Overcoming and Victory

A BIBLICAL STUDY

BY

DEBORAH KAISER LOOMIS

A wholly owned subsidiary of TBN

The Christian's Strategies for Overcoming and Victory
Trilogy Christian Publishers A Wholly Owned Subsidiary of Trinity
Broadcasting Network
2442 Michelle Drive Tustin, CA 92780

Rights Department, 2442 Michelle Drive, Tustin, CA 92780.
Trilogy Christian Publishing/TBN and colophon are trademarks of Trinity Broadcasting Network.
For information about special discounts for bulk purchases, please contact Trilogy Christian Publishing.

Trilogy Disclaimer: The views and content expressed in this book are those of the author and may not necessarily reflect the views and doctrine of Trilogy Christian Publishing or the Trinity Broadcasting Network.

Manufactured in the United States of America
10 9 8 7 6 5 4 3 2 1
Library of Congress Cataloging-in-Publication Data is available.
ISBN: 978-1-68556-109-3
E-ISBN: 978-1-68556-110-9

Dedication

To my husband of forty-two years, my two sons, their wives, and all my grandchildren: you are my abundant reward from the Lord!

> So let us seize and hold fast and retain without wavering the hope we cherish and confess and our acknowledgement of it, for He Who promised is reliable (sure) and faithful to His word.

Hebrews 10:23

Contents

Preface. 7

Prologue 9

Introduction. 11

The Strategies of the Enemy. 17

Strategy One. The Strategy of Praise 25

Strategy Two. The Strategy of Prayer 33

Strategy Three. The Strategy of Obedience 39

Strategy Four. The Strategy of Standing. 49

Strategy Five. The Strategy of

    Wrestling before God. 57

Strategy Six. The Strategy of Purity (Character). 65

Strategy Seven. The Strategy of Entering

    the Enemy's Camp 73

Strategy Eight. The Strategy of Humiliation

    or Humility 81

Strategy Nine. The Strategy of Love. 91

Strategy Ten. The Strategy of Anointed

    Single-Mindedness 99

Strategy Eleven. The Strategy of Thankfulness
/Thanksgiving 107

Strategy Twelve. The Strategy of the Table. 115

A Quick Review and Guide 123

Epilogue 125

Notes 127

Preface

This book was originally a series I taught for a women's Bible study. It was given to me by the Lord as I sat before Him, and in putting it forward into book form, I have tried to be faithful to how it was originally given to me by the Lord. I found it to have powerful tools for daily Christian living, and the women with whom I met regularly would testify along with me that we saw God work amazingly in our midst. Seeing these strategies put to work in the lives of actual Biblical examples gives us confidence in how God can work them in us. The Lord desires us to live in victory, over, not under, the enemy of our faith. My dearest prayer is that you have invited Jesus to be your Lord and Savior and that now, as you live with His Holy Spirit in you, this book would help you experience that victory daily.

Prologue

As a teacher of God's Word, I have a love for the Word that has transformed my relationship with Him. I find new things daily in the Scriptures to challenge me and encourage my walk with the Lord. Though my degree is in English and writing, I never thought to put all the teachings the Lord had given me into book form. That is exactly what the Lord called me to do after I had retired from my regular job. Truly, I never expected this, though I would be selfish to keep God's teaching to myself and from all the many in the Body of Christ who could be blessed by it. This book could be a tool in personal Bible study or can implement study with a group. My prayer is that no matter how God uses it, that it would bring great glory and honor to His name as His church is empowered for daily victory.

Introduction

When we begin to live as covenant people of God, Satan, our enemy, will engage us in a new way! He has more at stake now. Covenant blessing, by its very definition, means multiplication and extension of all God's goodness to generations! The devil hates this!

Whereas before, the enemy may have ensnared your foot, tripped you up, caused a stumble here and there, now that you have entered covenant life, he will engage you face-to-face, the ancient positioning in war. This is not to engender fear; remember, fear is *no part* of God's portion for His people. Rather, it is knowing your enemy as we, from the "higher places" of covenant life, can see and scout out his attempts to steal, kill, and destroy. And we go in armed with the knowledge that God has declared us overcomers of this evil one and his evil. Why? Because Jesus was and is the Overcomer, and in Him, *we are overcomers*. Praise God! The Trailblazer of our faith has become the *Trailblazer-Overcomer* that we may become in Him *many* trailblazer-overcomers. Amen!

Example One: Abraham

1. The declaration of the covenant blessing, the Word

(Genesis 12:1-3).

2. Receiving the covenant blessing (Genesis 12:4-8; temporary fear/regression in verses 10-20).

3. The harassment of the enemy (Genesis 13:70), often with family, separation from the old.

4. The reaffirmation of the covenant blessing (Genesis 13:14-16).

5. Abraham begins to walk in the covenant blessing (Genesis 13:17, 18).

6. Disturbance in the enemy's kingdom due to the move into covenant blessing (Genesis 14:1-12).

Ruling spirits revolt against ruling spirits. Evil spirit alliances are made to (1) steal, spoil (v. 11), and attack your wealth supply; (2) take cities (v. 11) and try to take territory: (3) touch your family, related individuals, and their goods!

1. Enemy's purpose in this is to engage you face-to-face, but don't back down! Go on the offensive; abandon the defensive position (v. 13). A *pursued* enemy!

2. Total victory results (v. 16)! Goods and people restored.

3. The communion at God's table, an affirmation of the

covenant that will stand (vv. 18-24).

Example Two: Joshua

1. Joshua and the people of Israel have entered the promised land and are *taking* it! Jericho and Ai have been taken; an alliance has been formed with Gibeon (albeit out of God's will).

4. Again, a disturbance is felt in the kingdom of evil: demonic rulers arise and form alliances (Joshua 10:1). The ruling factor here is *fear*. Again, we must choose to refuse fear! It provides a way for the enemy to operate. If Satan tries to get us to fear, we can never come into agreement with this! Remember, you can't operate in faith from a position of fear!

5. The enemy's purpose once again is to attack, confront, or engage Joshua and God's covenant people, Israel.

6. Enemy's strategy here is to attack those related, those in agreement with you (Joshua 10:5, 6). Notice the number of kings, *five*. The enemy will try to mimic the things of God. Here, he is using the number that often represents God's grace to mock God's purposes.

7. Joshua and the people of God *go on the offensive* and confront the enemy (v. 7).

8. Israel and Joshua hear the Word of the Lord and stand on it (v. 8).

9. Who fights? *God* (vv. 10-11)!

   - We pursue, confront, and stand. But *God* fights! It's *His* battle (v. 14)!

   - Become "God-inside-minded." When the enemy touches you, He touches God! The Anointed One and His anointing live within you, and the Word declares consequences to the enemy of God for doing this (Psalm 105:15).

10. Next, the enemy will try to hide. Even after the battle, do not give up or stop until *victory is seen completely.* Amen!

11. As you *stand*, you go on about everyday life, gaining victory in countless other ways (vv. 17-21). Unity is important at this time: no criticism of or comparison with others!

12. Put your foot on the enemy's neck. His neck is symbolic of the will of the enemy to destroy God's covenant people. As you do this, declare his end (vv. 24-25). Watch as God overcomes the enemy through you (v. 26).

13. Other enemy strongholds will fall as they hear about and fear you as God's covenant person (see the remainder of Joshua, chapter ten and Deuteronomy 28:7, 10).

Psalm 18:28-40

Psalm 18:33 (KJV): "He maketh my feet like hinds' feet." The female deer, or hind, follows the footsteps of her Hart, the Lord, as He ascends.

Psalm 18:33 (KJV): "[He] *setteth* me upon high places" (emphasis added). The Hebrew word here for "setteth" is *amad* (Strong's[1] #5975), which means to "stand," "abide," "appoint," "arise."

Notice the scripture sees us in "high places": over the enemy!

Psalm 18:34: the battle is the Lord's: all strategies for overcoming are *His*!

Psalm 18:35: defense is no concern of mine, for He is my Defender!

Psalm 18:37a: my position is to go forward! This involves the pursuit of the enemy. "I [...] overtook them" (Psalm 18:37a) or "took them over." The Hebrew word here is *nasag* (Strong's #5381), which means "reach," "be able," "attain," "can get," "remove," "take hold of, on, or upon."

Psalm 18:37b: no quitting until the enemy (sickness; poverty; assignments against your house, marriage, children; accidents, etc.) is gone! The Hebrew word here is *kalah* (Strong's #3615): to "end," "cease," "be finished," "perish," "make clean riddance."

Make no peace with the enemy of your soul!

Psalm 18:40: the enemy will *no longer* be able to engage you face-to-face! He will turn his back to you. *Why?* To flee!

The Psalm 18:40 (KJV) says, "Thou [Lord] hast also given me the necks of mine enemies." In other words, He has given their wills over to you! In God's strength and power, you have overcome them and their desire to thwart His covenant purpose, and that is the fullness of the blessing in your life!

Hallelujah! Amen!

The Strategies of the Enemy

John 10:10 says that the enemy's purpose is to steal, kill, and destroy!

Obviously, the enemy will attempt to deceive you so that he can destroy you. If you know him and his tactics for what they are, there would be no possibility that he could fool you! His only hope is deception.

Deception is subterfuge, or trickery. It also means to make an illusion, fraud, sham, being able to make a person believe as true something that is false.

Second John, chapter seven, references the "deceiver." The Greek word here is *planos* (Strong's #4108) and means "roving," "like a tramp," "by implication, an impostor or deceiver." See also the Strong's Hebrew #5377 used in Genesis 3:13, which means "beguiled" to reference the enemy's deception of Adam and Eve.

In Revelation 12:9, the Greek word used is *planao* (Strong's #4105), which means "to cause to roam, that is, from safety, truth, or virtue," "to go astray," "to wander," "to seduce."

If our enemy is deceptive and yet, at some point, engages us face-to-face to try to pull us out of covenant life, what are some of the strategies he uses?

Early on in your walk with the Lord, perhaps before you understood covenant living and God's will and inheritance for you in Christ Jesus, Satan's strategy against you most often was temptation. This was usually in the fleshly appetites or the "feelings." Old things that were set aside "reappeared" and now needed to be overcome anew.

Once the child of God in the covenant understands by the Holy Spirit that he or she does not live in his/her flesh or in his/her feelings, "but by every word that comes forth from the mouth of God," victory is obtained here! (Matthew 4:4, also Deuteronomy 8:3). Similarly, the covenant believer now knows that generational curses may try to reattach to him or her but that they have absolutely no authority to do so (Isaiah 53:5). Jesus paid the price for our wholeness on the cross; He was bruised for these generational sins to be broken off of us, so when they try to lay claim to us, we plead His Blood and declare the total provision of the cross.

Now, having moved on to the "higher places" with Him, we see the enemy, discern him as we have never been able to do before. He can't trip us up or snare our foot as before, so how will he operate?

Capture the Flag

Satan will attempt to encroach on your borders. He wants the territory you've acquired, as you have become an overcomer. This happened to the children of Israel after they took the land. The enemy will engage in "border skirmishes" to distract you and keep you from the Word and the Spirit (Joshua 19:47). The solution? Enlarge your territory! (See Jabez in 1 Chronicles 4:10; see also Isaiah 54:2, 3.) Don't give the enemy your territory: take *his*! If he dares to encroach on or touch the anointed of the Lord, the consequences are that he must give up his territory to you! Declare it (Deuteronomy 4:38; Proverbs 13:22)!

Make sure that you make no peace, agreement, or compromise with the enemy! The old saying "Give him an inch, he will take a mile" is rooted in Satan's character (Ephesians 4:26, 27). This will manifest itself in harassment, whether it is subtle or overt. Witchcraft or manipulation will be evidenced through strife with others, little sicknesses, or body ailments, even breaking down of appliances in the home. The enemy is trying to control you, to get you to submit to him. Immediately reject what is not of the Lord and His plan of blessing for you! Don't allow the encroachment!

The Blitz Attack

By its definition, this attack is a sudden, violent military campaign using many airplanes and tanks. In football, it is a play to pursue and attack the passer. Blitzkrieg is warfare in which the offensive is very rapid, violent, and hard to resist. One doesn't know where it will strike next! The word means "lightning war" in German. I think of this in spiritual warfare as sudden, violent attacks on many levels: accidents, sickness, financial hits, strife, etc. Satan's hope is to confuse you as well as to weaken you and wear you down. You're being hit on so many levels that you don't know where to start.

The solution? Start with the Word. Get it before your eyes, in your ears, in your heart, and on your lips! Don't worry about which battle to fight first! They all are no part of your covenant inheritance in Christ, so just begin to send out the Word. Counter with a blitzkrieg of your own using the Word of God, and it will hit the mark it needs to hit! Just decide not to faint or give up (Galatians 6:9; Isaiah 55:11; Jeremiah 1:12). Remember: it is the Lord who fights for you! Send the Word, and He will wield it for victory!

The Blame Game

In this tactic, the enemy attempts to accuse you: "All this is happening to me because I did something wrong." The Word of God says the accuser of the brethren, Satan, is a defeated foe! Send him to the throne to accuse you before

20

Jesus and then get on your knees. Examine your heart; ask the Holy Spirit to reveal any doors to sin that you may have opened. As He does, receive forgiveness, take a bath in the Blood of Jesus, and *go forward*! Don't listen to one more word of the enemy's lies.

If you examine yourself and ask the Holy Spirit to search out any sinful motives in yourself, know that your warfare is "such as is common to man" (1 Corinthians 10:13, KJV). You are in the world; you carry the seed of the anointing, and the enemy will try to come against you, but he cannot and will not succeed *if you don't let him*! Revelation 12:10-11 says we overcome with the Blood of Jesus, by the Word of our testimony (I say what God says!), and by loving not our lives unto the death (I humble myself, consecrating all I am and do to God).

Hide and Seek

Another strategy Satan will use is to attempt to conceal himself. As you battle him, you feel you get close to exposing him and his plan, and then he moves. Interestingly, the definition of "deceiver," as we learned before, means "to move about." First Peter 5:8 accurately describes the enemy on the move. As one with no peace, he keeps on moving. This is the opposite of one in Christ! That one is rooted, grounded, fixed, immovable (see 1 Peter 5:9)!

21

Know beyond a shadow of a doubt that the enemy cannot jump out and hurt you or what belongs to you. His hope is to get you to believe his growl, his seeming advantage (see Luke 10:19; Psalm 91:7, 10; John 16:33). He will be exposed! The light of Christ in you will shine on his darkness. Plus, as you resist him with what the Word declares, he *must* flee! It's a spiritual principle (James 4:7).

You counter his movement by standing firm in the Word and knowing who you are in Christ Jesus. Don't let his moving and hiding create havoc in your mind. (This is the only way he can get to you: in your thought parade.) Instead, renew your mind by the Word, take authority over non-God words, and refuse them (Romans 12:2).

Sympathy for the Enemy

Satan will attempt to become your companion to get you to look at things through his (the world's) eyes rather than through those of the Word. Don't make a bed with what is not of God! Be stern, ruthless with thoughts and imaginations that do not line up with God's Word.

Make no mistake: you may underestimate your enemy or say you have made peace with him, but it *will not* keep him from coming against you! You might say, "Oh, I have enough financially," or "I can live with this sickness/broken bone/disabled joint," or "This is just life." *Victory* is your portion in Christ! Expect it; hold out till you see it. Expect it *all* (2 Kings 13:17-19).

Now that we know our enemy and his tactics, as well as who we are in Christ, let's examine the twelve strategies God gives us for victory and overcoming the enemy.

Strategy One.

The Strategy of Praise

Jehoshaphat

Second Chronicles 20:1-30 highlights Jehoshaphat, whose name means "Jah is judge." If you also study chapter nineteen of the same book, you will see that Jehoshaphat, a king of Judah, learned what his name declared! As he lived within God's law and sought His righteousness, the Lord blessed him and Judah.

It is a spiritual principle that whenever you have moved up to a new position of authority in the Lord and that position has begun to affect others (2 Chronicles 19:4), the enemy will call you out "face-to-face." This happens for Jehoshaphat in 2 Chronicles 20:1-2. Not just one group, but three (!) come out against Jehoshaphat and the people: the Moabites, the Ammonites, and the Meunites.

The first response to such an attack?

1. Fear. Verse three says that "Jehoshaphat feared…" The word used here in Hebrew is *yare* (Strong's

#3372), which means "was frightened," "reverenced," "dreaded." His eyes, for a moment, were on the enemy and the threat attempted to move him. But...

2. Even though he had feared and acknowledged the enemy, he set himself to seek the Lord—a *decision*! In Hebrew, this is the word *nathan* (Strong's #5414): "gave," "committed," "applied," "appointed himself."

We might say that praise is "to say good things about; to give a good opinion of," "to worship, as in song."[2] "Seek" in Hebrew is *darash* (Strong's #1875) "to follow," "seek," "ask, specifically as applies to *worship*." Jehoshaphat made a decision to worship the Lord, to acknowledge that He is good and that He is all that is right! All this in the face of the enemy!

1. This is the first strategy of praise: turn from looking at the enemy and acknowledge that God is all that is good and all that you need!

Determine then that *all* your agreement is on that side: Jehoshaphat declared a fast for all the people, a setting apart of them to the side of God and His goodness.

Many of us, in a face-to-face confrontation with the

enemy, never get past this step because we don't turn from the situation or circumstance of the enemy to acknowledge *in his face* that the Lord is our God and that He is all that is good!

1. The second act of praise: we remind God of His covenant with us. Isaiah 62:6 reminds us "to put the Lord in remembrance [of His promises]" (brackets in the original).

    a. Declare who God is (2 Chronicles 20:6).

    b. Declare God is for us (vv. 7-9).

    c. Declare the enemy's purpose is to rob us of our inheritance (v. 10). Expose the thief!

    d. Turn to God, our covenant partner, and acknowledge that by coming against us, the enemy has come against God Himself (vv. 11-12). The enemy is touching the Anointed One and His anointing in you, and there are consequences for this. Ephesians 4:28 says, "Let the thief steal no more […]," and Proverbs 6:31 says, "But if he is found out, he must restore seven times [what he stole]."

2. The third act of praise: make room for the prophetic word!

    a. Wait for it (v. 13). Expect it to come!

    b. Know that it can come from anywhere and any*one*!

27

    c. Here in 2 Chronicles, chapter twenty, it comes through a worshipper, a son of Asaph. Asaph and his sons were psalmists, singers of worship songs of praise.

    d. The prophetic word gives life and hope and specifics for victory (vv. 15-16). Included in this is a strategy and exposure of the enemy's plan.

3. The fourth act of praise: the stillness of the Lord! "Stand ye still…" (2 Chronicles 20:17, KJV). Again, in Hebrew, it is *amad* (Strong's #5975); we learn this means "to stand," "abide behind [!]," "dwell," "continue." We live in this unmoved and unmovable place of the written and Spirit-declared word of the Lord! Hebrew *yataab* (Strong's #3320) is the word used here for "still" and means "to station yourselves," "place anything so as to stay," "offer," "continue." As you stay in the stillness, you will see the victory of the Lord (see also Isaiah 30:15 and Deuteronomy 28:7).

Here, *position* is all-important! Now God is between you and the enemy!

4. The fifth act of praise: out of the stillness comes the shout (v. 19) (see also Joshua 6: 10, 16-20 regarding the taking of Jericho). This has more to do with position than sound. Positioned worship brings forth the sound of victory! Now all this has happened, and yet the enemy has not been totally defeated. But now all is in God's hands, and

the enemy's defeat will be complete and total, as will be your blessing! At this point, many of us would say, "Well, the enemy's still there; he's not leaving." But don't give up or faint! The enemy's only hope is in us not pressing through to *total praise*.

5.   The sixth act of praise: walking it out!

6.   Like here, in 2 Chronicles 20:20, get up early in the morning and get going.

     a.   Stay in the declaration of the prophetic word (v. 20).

     b.   Now *sing* and praise God: tell Him who He is, declare His wondrous works to you in the past, and celebrate the victory *before* you've seen it (v. 21).

What happens here?

- The Lord sets up ambushments (traps, ways to expose, trip up, and slay) for the enemy. *God does it while you sing! And He does it completely!* In verse twenty-three, the enemies turn against each other and utterly destroy themselves. Once this enemy is consumed, you will not see him again (Exodus 14:13, 14).

- You get to see it (v. 24; also Psalm 27:13).

- You take home great spoil! The enemy isn't just

destroyed, but you now have what was his. Verse twenty-five here says it took them three *days* to gather the spoil. Wow!

7.   The seventh act of praise: you enlarge your borders to include a *new* place, the Valley of Blessing (Beracah). It's *celebration time*! What once was wilderness is now a place of blessing! The Hebrew word *berakah* (Strong's #1293) means "benediction," "prosperity," "pool," "blessings," "present." You now declare the place of the enemy's face-to-face confrontation to be the Valley of Blessing, now a place to evermore declare the goodness and love of almighty God, a testimony to *who God is*!

It's now a place of rejoicing over your enemies, a place of joy! Your joy is no longer dependent on your enemy, circumstances, situations, or people Satan attempts to use but on God Himself! You can *joy* because He is God, and *He is for you*!

8.   The final act of praise: the *stillness* moves from inside to out!

Now the enemy fears you because of your covenant partner, Jesus, and so stays far from you (v. 29; also Deuteronomy 28:10).

Jehoshaphat's realm was *quiet*! The Hebrew word here in verse thirty is *shaqat* (Strong's #8252), meaning "re-

30

pose," "at rest," "settled." God gave them *rest*! And the people of God lived here. Also, in verse thirty, the Hebrew word *nuwach* (Strong's #5117) is used. It implies a place "to rest," "settle," "dwell," stay."

The stillness God used to overcome the enemy—where the people of God themselves were still, but God was lifted up—now has made way for them to live in the place of *rest*. They can abide in the place of knowing who God is, that He is for them, and that He can and will overcome any enemy on their behalf. And *all this is ours, too, in Christ Jesus.* Make way for His victory in your life and prepare to live in the Valley of Blessing!

Amen!

Strategy Two.

The Strategy of Prayer

Genesis 18:17-33

Abraham

God's desire for you as an overcomer is to share *His* heart for the victory! See verse seventeen in this passage.

His promise: God won't hide what He desires/needs to do from you. You will know His will and what to pray. Why? Because like Abraham, you and I are God's friends and covenant partners! Galatians 3:1-9 tells us that we are heirs to this, as we are now in Christ Jesus through salvation in Him!

Verse eighteen: we, in Abraham, are those referenced here who carry the blessing. This agreement with God's heart, this union, was part of the purpose of God choosing you! And verse nineteen looks back on the original declaration of God's blessing to Abraham in Genesis 12:2-3.

Why did God choose Abraham (put your own name here!)? So that He could teach his children, even command them, so that God's heart/will could become part of your inheritance! The word used here in the original Hebrew is *tsavah* (Strong's #6680), which means to "constitute," "enjoin," "appoint," "charge," "give." In other words, Abraham (and you and I in Christ) can let our seed know that their inheritance is this union with God that brings forth the blessing!

We are the instruments of His blessing. Our agreement with God's heart, mind, and will is what gets His blessing and fullness to others, indeed, to the world!

The problem here, in this passage: Sodom and Gomorrah have become hotbeds of perversion and rebellion against God. God is moving to punish them for their sin. Abraham's nephew, Lot, has been dwelling here ever since he and Abraham divided up the land and took their respective family and herds to separate areas. In Genesis 18:20-22, we see that God (with the help of His two angels) is examining the situation. Note here that Satan is engaging God's covenant person, Abraham, by attacking those he loves, those who are related to him! This is a strategy we have previously studied the enemy using. But as always with the enemy, there are bigger implications than even the personal ones immediately at hand!

The strategy of prayer will keep you in the proper position for God to work.

1.   Remember, it's *His* battle, not ours (2 Chronicles 20:15; recall Jehoshaphat in our previous study of the strategy of praise).

Abraham stood still before the Lord (v. 22). Here in Hebrew, the word is *owd* (Strong's #5750), which means "iteration or continuance," "again," "repeatedly," "still more." The word here in the original text for "standing" or "was standing" is *amad* (Strong's # 5975), which means to "stand," "abide behind," "tarry," "appoint," "establish." In other words, set up camp here! Amen!

2.   Abraham stayed in his union with the Lord.
   a.   He was not moved by what God had revealed.
   b.   He was not moved by his own fears/concerns for Lot, his loved one.

3.   In fact, Abraham drew closer to the Lord (v. 23). He didn't move toward the situation either physically or mentally. He didn't run to Sodom and Gomorrah to save Lot himself, and he didn't begin to battle in his thoughts as to *how* to save Lot. Instead, he pressed into the Lord! The Hebrew here is *nagash* (Strong's #5066)" "to be or come near," "euphemistically, as to lie with a woman," "as an enemy, to attack," also, "to worship," "to approach." Abraham's attack against the enemy was in the drawing near to

God, in his worship and approach to the Lord. His forward motion now puts him in an offensive spiritual position!

The closeness of this strategy will allow heart-to-heart communion with God about the situation (vv. 23-25): Abraham reminded his covenant partner, God, who He is. He declared God's righteousness and judgment and justice.

God responded as a covenant partner (friend to friend), and Abraham was humbled! To think that the God of the universe could so love and hear him (vv. 26-27). We'll learn more about this strategy of humility later in this study.

Key! Abraham's refusal to let go until he sees the blessing of God, until he sees the situation that he is praying for, lines up to who he knows God to be! This makes all the difference (vv. 28-32).

Abraham kept on praying until he knew release, until God's covenant promises to him and his were as sure as if they had already manifested! Now, I believe that ten was the exact number of Lot's household. We know there was Lot, his wife, his two daughters and their husbands, and then, I believe, servants. I have no Biblical proof of this, just a Holy Spirit hunch that this is the reason that the number ten (the ten righteous ones he asked to be found there) gave Abraham his release!

The release of the blessing frees God to work now as the account continues in Genesis, chapter nineteen.

1. There is judgment for those outside the covenant.

2. Salvation and a way of escape are provided for those who are related in the covenant, here, Lot and his household.

3. Please note that free will is still in operation! Lot's sons-in-law thought his urging to flee the city was a joke (Genesis 19:14); Lot's wife disobeyed the angels by looking back on what she was leaving and so became a pillar of salt (Genesis 19:17, 26), and even Lot's own pleas regarding their destination had future consequences for his own daughters.

Job 22:30 says that, through our intercession, God will save those who are not innocent. (Genesis 19:29). But then He will still look to draw them into a personal covenant agreement with Himself, and this is up to them! In verse twenty-nine, God remembers His covenant partner, Abraham. The Hebrew word here is *zakar* (Strong's #2142), meaning to "mark," "remember," "mention," "be mindful of."

Daniel 10:1-21 tells us that there was warfare in the heavenlies the moment Daniel's intercession began. At that very time, warfare had begun over the very matter for which Daniel prayed. Your obedient agreement with God and His purposes, heart, will, and mind looses:

1. heavenly warfare on behalf of the people and situation you pray for;

2. strategy for you;

3. refreshment for your spirit and soul that may be overcome temporarily by the attack (Daniel 10:19);

4. more prophetic revelation.

5. Finally, friends, be strengthened in prayer! Know the sure victory of obedience in agreement with your Lord, the Overcomer, the Victor!

Amen!

Strategy Three.

The Strategy of Obedience

Moses

The third strategy for overcoming and victory, which we will examine, is that of obedience. The word "obey" is defined as "to do what one is told." It comes from the Latin *oboedire* (*ob* meaning "to"; *audire*—"to listen," "give ear"). The word implies really hearing and receiving! So, how does obedience deliver you from face-to-face attack from Satan, the enemy of our souls?

It puts you in the place of agreement with the Word! This is making "yourself inaccessible" to the enemy, as it says in Psalm 91:8. This psalm also talks about being in the "secret place." Why is it secret? Because not everyone knows about it! In this place, the enemy may be able to see and observe you, but he may not touch you! Sometimes, he is not even able to see or hear you! Darkness hides you, or the cloud and fire of His presence, just as He did for the Israelites as they traveled to the promised land. Psalm 143:9 says when the enemy pursues us, we flee to the Lord to hide us! Amen!

Our scripture for this strategy is Exodus 3:1-22: the example of Moses.

Moses's name comes from the Hebrew *mosheh*, Strong's #4872, meaning "drawing out (from the water)"; "i.e., rescued." And if you recall the story of how he was drawn out of the water after being placed there for his protection by his natural mother, he is the perfect picture of us in Christ Jesus! Like Moses, we are chosen, rescued, and preserved in Christ.

The Call to Covenant Life

Moses was just doing his everyday work when he came to the mountain of God, Sinai (Exodus 3:1). There, God (the Angel of the Lord, *Jesus*!) appeared to him in a burning bush. Note that the bush was burning but was not being consumed. That would catch my attention! This is a caution to us to pay attention to what is beside and around us, as there may be a revelation of God in it for us! For Abraham, it was a ram in the thicket; for Moses here, a burning bush!

The Lord used the unusual (the nonconsuming burning) to get Moses to pay attention to Him. Watch for this: God will work in the same way for you and me! Be alert in the spirit for the unusual!

God calls Moses by name here. He establishes that He knows him familiarly, intimately. And Moses responds! Most likely, Moses and God have become intimate through all those years of sheep tending and exile (forty [!] years). He responds, "Here I am!"

This is the first touchstone of obedience! "Here I am, Lord, available to hear, receive, and obey Your Word. My ears are Yours, Lord, given to Your words!"

Now comes an encounter in holiness: As God reveals Himself, we see who we are in relation and response to the revelation. God says, "Get ready for some new shoes when I knock you out of your old ones!" Wow! Please notice that holiness has life and action attached to it, not a "being ready" to be placed on a shelf and admired!

God declares Moses's (and our!) inheritance through his forefathers, Abraham, Isaac, and Jacob (v. 6) as He reveals His plan. He announces the provision, promises, and prosperity He has for Moses and the people of God (v. 8). God declares His purpose for Moses (v. 10).

Again, Moses sees and notes his inability (v. 11). We, too, will feel this way as God prepares us for victory. Just don't *stay* here!

God says, "I *will be with you* in your inability. What

I need is your *availability*!" And God tells Moses He will confirm it with a sign. God delights to confirm His word!

In Exodus 3:14 comes the revelation of His Name, I AM THAT I AM! I heard Gloria Copeland teach on this years ago, and she noted the emphasis on the *THAT*. In other words, God reminds Moses He is *THAT I AM*, the one who gave these promises to his forefathers, Abraham, Isaac, and Jacob. He's saying to Moses that He hasn't forgotten or abandoned Moses and the people of God. His very reminder stirs faith that He will bring them into their promised inheritance!

God tells Moses to remind His people that He has made a deposit of Himself in them through the previous visitation and that He is watching over that deposit to protect and deliver them, as well as bring it forth (v. 16). God says that what this enemy has done to them, it has done to Him!

The Lord prepares Moses for his face-to-face encounter with the enemy and how that enemy will resist God's purposes and plan—*strategy* (vv. 18-19)!

God says, "Fear not! I will overcome this enemy, and he will flee and get out of My plan for you." And God promises here that He will also give them the enemy's goods, so they don't just get released, they get prosperity (vv. 20-22). Moses gets the message that his confrontation with the enemy and ultimate victory is for the freedom and prosperity of *many*!

The Authority of the Word: "How do we fight?" (Exodus 4)

God says, "What is that in your hand?" (Exodus 4:2). Moses replies that he has a rod in his hand. The rod symbolizes the Word of God. It's what protects and guides us as He draws us to Himself. But it is also powerful against the enemy! If you have anything else in your hand with which to do battle besides the Word, let it go! Deuteronomy 30:14-15 says that what you need for overcoming is right in your grasp. It is His Word in you, in your heart, if you've been diligent to put it there. Then grab it and wield it!

God demonstrates His authority and sovereignty with signs and wonders as we yield what we have to Him. Interestingly, Acts 7:22 (KJV) tells us that Moses "was mighty in words and deeds," so his inability was not true. He was just afraid. God stirs us to overcome our fear!

God Reminds Moses That the Battle is the Lord's (vv. 10-17)

All our objections, confessions of inadequacy matter not! God is looking for that one positioned in His authority and carrying the authority of God's Word (vv. 17, 20).

God tells us the enemy won't go willingly, but *He will*

43

go (v. 21). God tells Moses to prophesy the enemy's end up front. In verses twenty-two and twenty-three, God tells Moses to tell the pharaoh that his seed will be destroyed if he does not let the seed of God go. Again, God reminds the enemy not to touch what is His. This is a promise to claim and declare!

The Lord will search you out to make sure that your obedience is total, that the enemy finds nothing with which to accuse you (vv. 24-27; also Psalm 139:23-24). You just receive His forgiveness and correction as things come up in the examination. Then line up, go forward, and God will minister to you (vv. 26-28).

The enemy will attempt to make you give up the confrontation with him and see the "old thing" as more comfortable and less dangerous. Often others will press you to turn back, to leave it alone. In chapter five of Exodus, the enemy's pressure makes the hearts of Moses and the people of God faint. Their burden, it seems, has only increased instead of them seeing deliverance.

But don't faint! This is the enemy's only hope! He fears you and God in you and knows he can only continue the captivity if you back off! Deliverance is sure even though it tarries! Know that God requires this of you for His kingdom to come. Disobedience will not keep you safe; being

44

in God's will is the safest place to be!

You are *as God* to the enemy! As you speak and stand, the enemy sees Jesus (Exodus 7:1).

The enemy will attempt to counterfeit the miracles of God but will be overcome every time (Exodus 7:10-21). Here, Egyptian magicians tried to counter Moses and Aaron with serpents and by turning the Nile to blood. Interestingly, in the latter, the magicians imitated what Moses, through God, had done rather than reverse it and so punished the Egyptians with no water to drink. The enemy has no actual power to overcome you as God's covenant person. He relies on counterfeit imitation to deceive.

There are plagues all around you as you stand before the enemy, secure in obedience to the Word of God. These are the judgments of God against the enemy and the world serving him because he will not bow the knee to almighty God in you:

1. river to blood,

2. frogs,

3. gnats,

4. gadflies,

5. livestock plague,

6. boils,

7. hail,

8. locusts,

9. darkness,

10. slain firstborns.

The enemy will try to get you to compromise on God's plan for complete deliverance: in Exodus 8:25, he tried to tell them *where*. In Exodus 10:8-11, he tries to tell them *who* and *with whom*. In Exodus 10:24, he tries to say *with what*. The enemy will try to control God's plan for full victory, but make no compromises! Obey completely!

The protection of you as God's person will be complete! In Exodus 8:23, God places a division, a barrier between the enemy and us! Here in the original Hebrew, the word is *peduth* (Strong's #6304), which means "a distinction," "a redemption." Wow! See Exodus 9:7, 26, and 10:23. Obedience and trust save you from every tactic of the enemy!

1. God provides here a lamb for a household (Exodus 12:3, 11). This signified their redemption and salvation.

2. The provision of the Blood (Jesus's blood shed for you) provides absolute safety for you and your seed

(Exodus 12:13, 14, 23).

Why the delay? Why not immediate victory? Because God gets *great glory*, and you get memorials to show the enemy the next time he confronts you and God's life in you. *Wow*! When he attacks, declare those memorials and send the enemy to look at them! See Deuteronomy 7:16-24.

God's people come forth from the confrontation with the enemy in fullness and with overflowing (Exodus 12:35, 36). What was the enemy's is now yours!

You now have guidance and revelation to move forward. For the Israelites, it was the cloud by day and the fire by night (Exodus 13:21, 22; Exodus 14:19, 20).

You have a memorial! The Israelites had Passover. We have Communion, the table of God (more to come on this in strategy #12). Here you have someplace to go where the enemy cannot touch you.

Deliverance is complete; there is no enemy anymore (Exodus 14:13-15). So now...*go forward to covenant blessing and life!*

Amen!

Strategy Four.

The Strategy of Standing

1 Samuel 30

David

David, anointed by God to rule and reign (like us in Christ), has been moving into the fullness of the mantle God has for him to wear. The enemy, Satan, has observed this as well as the move of the current king of Israel, Saul, toward destruction, and so the devil attacks.

1. The enemy will try to bring captivity to your life. You've declared your freedom in the Lord, so now the devil tries to bring captivity to you!

He will appear to "tie up" those who belong to you, as well as touch what belongs to you (1 Samuel 30:1-3). You've been "about the battle," and the enemy does this while you are so occupied. But notice: David's preoccupation would have taken him to war against Israel, so God preserved him from this. He had been running from Saul and taken refuge amongst the Philistines. No agreement, however, is possible with what is not of God! You can't fight with that! When God plucks you out of the place to which you have run for refuge, and you pursue agreement with Him only, then you are ready for restoration. God is always working to save us from ourselves!

1. It's okay to cry! Notice this in verse four of chapter thirty. Psalm 103:14 says that God remembers that we are but dust. The Hebrew word used here is *aphar* (Strong's #6083), which means "clay," "earth," in other words, created, human! Hebrews 4:15 reminds us that Jesus understands this because He, too, became like us and experienced the weaknesses, frailties, and emotions of the flesh. He understands and sympathizes! Psalm 56:8 says that God records and is mindful of our tears. We just can't stay here!

2. The enemy will attempt to distress you by others who have looked to you or stood with you but are now turning from you. Verse six here in 1 Samuel, chapter thirty, says David experienced this. The men under his leadership blamed him for their common losses. The Amalekites had come to their camp, burned it, and had taken all their women and children and servants captive. David was grieving

his losses, too, but his companions reacted with anger and blame and sought to kill him. Scripture says David was distressed, in the Hebrew language, *yatsar* (Strong's #3334), which means he was "pressed," "made narrow," "in narrow straits." Obviously, this is the opposite of God's will for you in Christ Jesus. He says He will bring you into large, broad, pleasant places, full of freedom! If it doesn't look like God, it's not!

The enemy's plan is not only to kill, steal, and destroy those who and what belongs to you, but he's after your life, too! He is trying to press you down into narrow places—into the cracks, you might say—so that you are ineffective for covenant blessing and victory.

Be alert: the devil may use friends to do this! Be aware that the enemy has put fear on them, which is the root of their pressing you. He has lied to them and "bitterly grieved" them, as says 1 Samuel 30:6. Remember that bitterness is anger pushed deep down into the soul, a belief that God is not for me. This is the devil's lie!

Bless your friends and go forward!

1. What does David do here, and what are we to do? It says in verse six that "David encouraged [...] him-

self in the Lord." In Hebrew, the word used here is *chazaq* (Strong's #2388). It means "to fasten upon," "to seize," be "strong," "strengthened," "courageous," "bound to," "cleave to." This is one of my favorite words in the whole Hebrew language! David fastened himself onto the Lord his God for dear life and said, "Devil, you're not moving me! I know God has anointed me as His covenant person, and I will fulfill my destiny in Him. All that is mine will be restored and then some." Wow!

As we fasten ourselves onto God and *stand unmoved* in His presence, His Word, His power, we acknowledge *who He is* and so remind ourselves *who we are in Him*!

How do we do this? Well, you get in the presence of God! In verse seven, David went to the priest and got the ephod, the high priest's symbol that signified he could approach the ark of the covenant and be in the presence of God. David didn't ask Abiathar, the priest, to do this for him—he did it himself! This is a shadow of our substance in Christ! We can freely approach our heavenly Father because we stand by the shed blood of Jesus.

1. While standing in this place, David seeks God's strategy, not his own!

In verse eight, he decides to refuse his fleshly impulses, what he himself would do. God replies with what David should do and assures him of the victory!

Principle: when we give up our right to know what to do and, instead, seek God's way, two things happen: (1) we get specific guidance; here, it was simple: pursue! And (2) we get a guarantee of success and victory.

1. So now, we go forward with those in agreement with us and God's Word in us! Let the Lord sort this out. He will! Not everyone went with David on this recovery and restoration mission.

Here, in 1 Samuel 30:9-10, they came to the brook Besor, which means "cold."[3] Matthew 24:12-13 says some hearts will grow cold. When that happens, they can't endure. They want to give up or quit. God will cause you to be separated from the "giver-uppers" if you agree with His victory!

These ones who grow "cold" are exhausted and faint. Hebrew here is *pagar* (Strong's #6296) "to relax," i.e., "to become exhausted, be faint." This is not a condemnation! It's merely a commentary. Their flesh has failed them and caused them to be worn out, unable to endure and go forward. It's dangerous for them to go!

1. So David pursued and went forward with the 400 men who were able. Hebrew *radaph* (Strong's #7291) means "to run after," "to chase," "to put to flight," "follow after," "hunt." This is an offensive tactic; they are *not* on the defense here.

David's obedience to the Word of God, not deterred by others, but still going forward after the enemy, bears fruit immediately (vv. 11-15).

God supplies revelation and exposure of the enemy through an unlikely source, an Egyptian! He tells them he is a servant to the Amalekites who raided their camp and stole from them and that he knows where they are!

Principle: keep your eyes open because you never know how God is going to give a continuing strategy or exposure of the enemy. Be alert! Don't refuse it because the source looks unlikely!

1. God's means of revelation will take you right into the enemy's camp. The enemy will be unsuspecting, gloating in his seemingly successful thievery. Remember, the devil is *not* omniscient, omnipotent, or omnipresent. Only God is all those things! Satan relies on demons to relay what they observe, and when you are in line with God's strategy for victo-

ry, the eyes and ears of the enemy are shut. You are hidden with Christ in God (Psalm 27:5; Colossians 3:3). Amen!

2. Your victory will be *absolutely complete* (vv. 17-19). *All* was recovered by David and his men: nothing missing, nothing broken—*shalom*! (See Psalm 23:1.)

3. Your borders will be *enlarged* (v. 20). *Principle*: God will not only return all that was taken from you, but you shall have what is the enemy's!

4. God's victory over the enemy humbles you so that you have a heart for others (vv. 21-23).

David *saluted* the 200 men who had given up and waited by the brook Besor. The word here in Hebrew is *shalom* (Strong's # 7965). Literally, he asked of them their peace. In other words, he inquired as to their wholeness, "How can I help you become whole where you are broken?" *Wow*!

David speaks his humility and compassion in the face of those who would want to curse instead of blessing. The men who went with him were not inclined to share God's blessing with these ones. But David gently corrected them (vv. 23-25).

Principle: God's blessings will always put you in the

position to extend them to others and should give you the desire to do so!

David declares what these men want to do (keep all the spoil for only those who went to battle) doesn't line up with God and His Word. He says, "Who would listen to you in this matter?" (1 Samuel 30:24).

Principle: the victory in battle always has corporate benefits, even if the victory seems individual. It's for the Body of Christ and the purposes of God's kingdom!

1. God's victory positions you for the anointing to come forth in *fullness* and *overflow* (vv. 26-31).

David blesses the people of Judah, even those who previously had denied him refuge, and so prepares the way for his occupation of the throne of Israel, fulfilled in 2 Samuel 2:4.

How has the enemy stolen from you? God asks you to stand, fastened onto Himself, and as you do, the victory will be sure! You will be blessed, *all* will be restored, those who were giving up will be strengthened anew, and even those who condemned you before will make way for God's kingdom to come—in you and in the world!

Amen!

Strategy Five.

The Strategy of Wrestling

before God

Genesis 32:1-32

Jacob

Jacob comes out from captivity and oppression into covenant life. He's positioned for covenant life after leaving the seeming security and familiarity of Laban. That false covenant let him be used and deceived from realizing the fullness of his inheritance. Immediately, he is met by an army of angels and becomes two companies: *Mahanaim* (v. 2). This word in Hebrew signifies two armies.

1. True knowing of your inheritance denotes sonship and daughtership and calls down the heavenly forces to join you. You become a double company: you + God's angels!

2. This brings boldness to cause restoration for others,

in this case, Esau (vv. 3-6).

3. *Fear* will still try to stop you here, but don't let it!
    Refuse it! Satan uses fear to keep you from victory
    in new things.

4. Jacob attempts to plan to save himself (vv. 7-8).

God reminds Jacob what is in his hand, what has
brought him thus far: *the Word of God* (vv. 9-10). *The Word
brought him out, and the Word will save him and bring
him into fullness*! Remembering the Lord's Word humbles
Jacob before God.

Jacob recalls how the flocks multiplied. This was
revelation knowledge! God gave him the wisdom to know
how to multiply the flocks. He *knows* God is his substance!
The word he recalls here, in Hebrew, is *maqqelah* (Strong's
#4731): "staff," "germinate," "a shoot, i.e., a stick (with
leaves on, or for walking, striking, guiding, divining),"
"rod," "hand staff." This is what supports Jacob! The rod
before the animals transformed them into his inheritance,
much to Laban's consternation.

God's Word has brought him (and us!) *out and over*.
God's Word has caused Jacob to "double." His father, Isaac,
had known the double in Gerar (Genesis 26), and then he
produced the double: Jacob and Esau, twins!

Jacob sees this enemy from the past (his brother whom he had cheated out of the blessing) as confronting and threatening him.

1. He's still operating in the old thing.

2. Jacob reminds God of His promises to him (by the way, God loves this).

3. Although he is afraid, fear doesn't move him; faith does: in verse thirteen, he prepares a gift for his brother. This may have been to appease, but I believe there is a genuine desire in Jacob to bless Esau out of his own blessing!

Principle: when fear threatens, cut it off by giving to others.

1. Faith is evident in Jacob's desire for the relationship.

Fear would appease and flee, but faith gives and loves!

Faith and fear are still at war in Jacob; this is evidenced by his trying to protect his own seed and spouses (vv. 22-23). God needs to address this in His covenant man or woman.

There can be *no compromise* with fear, the past, and the old covenant, or God cannot bring forth the fullness of overcoming victory that Jesus died and rose again to give us.

Key: in covenant life, you forever give up the right to save and take care of yourself!

Jacob meets a Man, that is, Jesus; the Son of Man and God comes to wrestle with Jacob. Hebrew here is *abaq* (Strong's #79), "to float away as vapor," but also used as denominative #80, "to be dust," i.e., "grapple," "wrestle." Hebrew #80 is *abaq*, meaning "light particles," "dust." In other words, Jesus here was grappling with the flesh in Jacob, the old man, the Adamic covenant. This is not ours anymore if we are in Christ!

Hebrew *iyah* (Strong's # 376) means "a man," "a mighty man," "a champion," "a husband" (!). His champion, our champion, Jesus, and our husband, as we are His Bride, comes to Jacob and grapples with the fleshly nature in him and in us!

Key: the old birth is through God's son Adam. The new blessing is through the second born, Jesus, but firstborn of the Father. Then is ushered in the true birthright and blessing, the double-double!

There is resistance in Jacob and in us! Hebrew *yakol* (Strong's #3201) means he did not "*prevail*," "be able," "overcome," "have power," "could not." (Because Jacob would not. Yet!)

What does God do? He touches his joint! The Interlinear Bible says, "He touched his hip socket, and his hip socket was unhinged" (Genesis 32:25, paraphrased). Hebrew *yarrek* (Strong's #3409) means "the thigh," "the generative parts," "shank," "flank," "side," "body," "loins." Where did Eve come out of Adam? Where was Jesus pierced with a spear? His side...

"Generative" implies having to do with the production of offspring, the producing parts. In other words, the intimate place between his thighs, the "hollow"! Hebrew for this is *kaph* (Strong's #3709): "the hollow of a palm," "figuratively, power," "handled."

God places His powerful, authoritative touch upon the multiplying part of Jacob! (And us...) Wow! What happens when God touches us? We are forever different! Life goes from Him into us, and something new is created! Hallelujah!

Jacob knows something is different but asks the Lord to declare it over him: the blessing! God says He will do that if Jacob tells him his name (Genesis 32:27). In other words, how do you identify yourself, Jacob? *Como te llamas?* How do you call yourself? *By* what are you known?

This stuns Jacob and us into self-revelation and realization! "I have been calling myself on my own! It's been all about me!" Jacob replied, "Jacob" (Strong's #3290): "heel-catcher, supplanter." In other words, he says, "I've been the one trying to get this inheritance myself. I cheated and deceived to get what I thought was the blessing, but it wasn't!"

Immediately, God (Jesus) rushes to restore him in verse twenty-eight. He tells Jacob that he may now realize that's what he was, but God's blessing now declares *who he is in Him, Israel*! Jacob's new name comes from the Hebrew *Yisrael* (Strong's #3478), which means "he will rule as God."

Why? Because Jacob had contended with God and with himself. The word here in Hebrew is *sarah* (Strong's #8280), which means "prevailed," "have power as a prince." Wow! God is saying, "Now you know you are My son!" Jacob has been "overshadowed" in his birthing parts, and now he can bring forth what is of God (see Luke 1:35).

Jacob then cries out for God to reveal *His* name to him. His own name, his own fleshly nature, is no longer important. He realizes he is called by God's own name, and Jacob desires to know the fullness thereof!

This is the cry of a son or daughter to know his/her inheritance!

God's answer to Jacob? To bless him! He poured Himself out over him there (v. 29).

Jacob names the place Peniel, which means "face of God." His understanding now is that God has imparted Himself to him, face-to-face, right while the enemy (the old thing) was to engage him, and though there has been a death to his fleshly nature, he *lives*! He has never been more alive and full of hope.

And as Jacob goes forward, he *limps*; Hebrew here is *tsala* (Strong's # 6760), which means "to curve," "to limp as if one-sided," "halt." It's like a personal memorial that he is now only on one side, God's, and all God's blessing is in him! In other words, he leans God's way only and depends on Him! A God-joined three-legged race comes to mind.

The limp and lesson Jacob learned are also a corporate memorial to Israel and the church.

Have we allowed God to wrestle our fleshly nature and mark us in our multiplying, intimate spots? If so, our flesh may be halt or lame, praise God, but our spirits will be strong in the Lord! Called by His name only, refusing all else, the Bride will be adorned with the beautiful full gown of His inheritance (it covers her halt flesh!) and covenant life. And so, His glory covers the limping part of us. All who see the Bride will stand and exclaim and give glory to God!

Hallelujah and amen!

Strategy Six.

The Strategy of Purity

(Character)

Job 22:21-30

Job

Matthew 5:8 says that the pure in heart shall see God.
The word "heart" here in Greek is *kardia* (Strong's #2588),
which means "the heart," "thoughts," "feeling," "the mid-
dle." The word in Greek for "pure" is *katharos* (Strong's
#2513), which means "clean," "clear." In other words, as in
Ephesians 5:26, it means everything we think, feel, and are
motivated by is washed by the water of the Word!

Now, how is this a strategy against the enemy? When
the enemy gets in your face, when he faces off with you,
purity, this cleanness of heart or *charakter* in the Greek
language (which in Greek means "an exact likeness or
engraving of"), makes you look like God and puts the devil

to flight.

It is a strategy of heart that transforms your situation and circumstances!

In the book of Job, we find the keys to purity, to having the character of God (being in His express image), clean, cleansed of all there is of our flesh.

1.   Verse twenty-one here begins by telling us to acquaint ourselves with Him. Job's friend Eliphaz is counseling Job in the midst of his oppression. The Hebrew here is *cakan*, pronounced [saw-kan] (Strong's # 5532), which means "to be familiar with," "minister to," "be serviceable to," "to cherish," "be customary."

In other words, seek God, find out who He is, and agree only with that and Him!

How do I do this?

a.   His Word reveals Him.

b.   Nature declares and shows Him (Psalm 19:1-4a).

c.   His Spirit reveals to us all the truth of who He is (John 16:13-15).

As God reveals Himself to you, you respond, just as Abraham did when God revealed Himself through His different names! And remember, it can't be God if it doesn't agree with who the Word reveals Him to be. What is our response as the strategy against the enemy? I agree with who God is (see Matthew 18:18-20); I know He is I AM, and I agree with Him—spirit, soul, and body! The enemy will be defeated before your face when you agree with Him as I AM! In Matthew 14: 23-32, we read the account of the disciples in the boat when the storm arose. Their fear caused them to cry out and question Jesus's care. Like them, we say, "Look at the winds and waves, Lord! Stop them!" But Jesus says, "You look to Me, and the winds and the waves will submit to us, you and Me!" Amen!

2.   Having looked to who God is, now choose wholeness of body, soul, and spirit. Decide that this is God's will for you and accept nothing else. We are still in verse twenty-one, and it says in the Amplified Bible, Classic Edition, that we "agree with God" and show ourselves "to be conformed to His will [...] and be at peace." The word here in Hebrew is *shalam* (Strong's # 7999) and means "be safe," "be made completed," "to be at peace," "to prosper." The Hebrew word *shalom* comes from this root. Jews greet each other with this word, declaring they want the other to be whole and well. I heard Gloria Copeland say to think of it as "nothing missing, nothing broken." The enemy would have no shot at us if we refused anything of him and the world and would only receive what is of God, that which

makes us whole and complete (see also 2 Timothy 3:17, Ephesians 5:17).

We cannot believe God's will for us is anything less than His Word says it is!

3. If you do steps one and two, Job 22:21 says, "Good shall come to you." In other words, good will seek you out! You will be surrounded with good; good will go to work for you, and this includes angels! Now, angelic forces are loosed (the double company, angels and us, the *mahanaim* we learned about with Jacob) to fight with you against the evil one and his evil purposes. The devil's end is sure!

4. Verse twenty-two: again, go to the Word! *Word, Word, and more Word*! Get His instruction from Scripture and from His Spirit; keep it before your eyes and *seal* it to your heart! If you do this, the enemy can never defeat you or gain any advantage over you before the *Word* rises up in you on every occasion and in every circumstance. Don't wait until he's in your face to do this, but if you are at that place, it's never too late! As you loose God's Word, He goes to work to perform it (Jeremiah 1:12). Amen!

5. Verse twenty-three: keep going back to your source, the Lord! "Return," it says here: turn again to Him! Get your eyes off yourself and your circumstances. This is humbling yourself. You cannot save yourself! The devil absolutely cannot work with a character like this that looks

like God. Humility, as when Jesus humbled Himself to go to the cross, or God's love in sending His only Son to atone for us, confuses the devil because it is foreign to his nature! Remember, what brings forth fruit is agreement. If you agree with God, you will see victory. But make no mistake: the enemy is looking for your agreement too. Don't give it to him!

God says your decision to *constantly keep turning back to look at Him and who He is* will build you up in your inner man. It will put unrighteousness and the author of unrighteousness far from your tents. Hallelujah! The devil won't be able to live near you.

6. Verses twenty-three to twenty-seven: declare that God is your supply, and only God! Then back it up with a demonstration.

> a. Pursuit of prosperity on a fleshly level can corrupt you and open a foothold to the enemy. This is trying to lay hold of your inheritance in Christ by yourself. (Like Jacob did!)
>
> b. Examine yourself and see if only the Lord is your gold and silver. This is demonstrated by where your money goes and what motivates you in your life.
>
> c. Giving, giving, giving! We undo the devil in this simple way. When you give, you are resisting

the devil and coming into agreement with God, and so the enemy is commanded by the Word to flee from you and your concerns (James 4:6-7).

d. Also, when you give, it puts you in a position for face-to-face communication and delight with the Almighty (v. 26). The Hebrew for "delight" is *anaq* (Strong's #6026), which means "to be soft or pliable," "have delight in." There is the implication of intimacy as in how a wife is with her husband. There's no chance for the devil to face off with you in such a position.

e. Answered prayer will be the norm for you! You will have God's heart and mind as you pray and agree with Him, and what you pray will be done (v. 27). See also James 5:16b. There's power here: when your heart is cleansed and set apart to Him, He can do His will on the earth through you, in you, and for you! And here, it mentions vows. What are your vows? Only to love and seek Him with all your heart! (In Micah 6:8, Deuteronomy 10:12, and Matthew 22:37-40, we are told what God requires of us.)

7. Verses twenty-eight and twenty-nine: you will exercise your authority and dominion, which is *His* in you, over all situations and circumstances.

You will constantly call things into line with the Lord and His will in you and for you.

God's favor will be on everything you do! It will evidence itself everywhere you turn. And the devil flees at the sight of God's favor and you calling down His will because if God is for us, who can be against us (Romans 8:31)?

The very act of the enemy attempting to put you under his feet, his control, will cause the declaration to rise up in you. "There is a lifting up" (Job 22:29). In other words, what the devil means for evil, God will turn to good! "I am not under the curse but under the blessing."

This is a true submission, a humbling yourself to God's will (which is *all* good) for you, and so He will save you and lift you up. As you lift Him up and refuse to save yourself (which is the devil's appeal to your flesh), He will then lift you up and cause you to prosper and succeed.

8. Verse thirty: a new level of intercession will be birthed in and through you!

As God does this in you, and His character and purity cause the devil to flee from you, you will have the authority to pray the same for others. This is even for those who haven't come to this place yet themselves! God's character, when it is written on our lives by the pierced palms of

Jesus, by His death and resurrection life, can declare life for those even not yet open to it. We can call things that be not as though they already were (Romans 4:17) and see many brought to salvation and wholeness.

As always, God's shalom in you has kingdom shalom in mind also! Will you let God's shalom begin in you by allowing Him to be Himself in you to the world?

In Revelation 12:11, God says we are overcomers by:

a. the Blood of the Lamb: our covenant position in Christ;

b. the word of our testimony: our covenant portion/ inheritance in Christ;

c. that we loved not our lives unto the death: our covenant purity in Christ.

When Christ is all and in all, the enemy cannot stand!

Amen!

Strategy Seven.

The Strategy of Entering the Enemy's Camp

Judges 6–7

Gideon

The background:

God makes a covenant with Gideon, a man of the Israelite tribe of Manasseh. Gideon's name (in Hebrew, *Gidown*; Strong's #1439) means "a feller, "one who cuts down," "a warrior."

1.   Judges 6:11-12: the Angel of the Lord (Jesus) comes and declares His agreement with Gideon. See verse twelve: "The Lord is with you." As with Joseph, etc.: this is a covenant phrase!

2.   The Lord declares how *He* sees Gideon. "You mighty man of [fearless] courage" (Judges 6:12) or "valor" (KJV). Yet Gideon is displaying just the opposite! He is in

fear of the Midianites, and he is hiding wheat.

Principle: when God meets you in covenant life, He always declares you to be who you are in Him, not who you appear to be in the circumstances!

3. God then declares the purpose of His covenant life in Gideon: to save many and turn them *all* to His covenant blessing (vv. 13-14).

4. Gideon continues to focus his declaration on the natural (v. 15). We all do this!

5. God (so very patient is He!) reiterates the covenant blessing (v. 16) (as He did before to Abraham, Isaac, and Jacob). In the face of our fear, He builds our faith!

6. The covenant meal: here, it is prepared by Gideon and then consumed (not eaten!) by God as a demonstration of agreement (vv. 17-22). Just like in the old covenant, the flesh is consumed by fire. We partake of Him (His death on the cross and resurrection as portrayed by the bread and cup), and He partakes of us (as we become broken bread and poured out wine).

7. The God of peace: Jehovah Shalom (v. 24). Gideon understands and receives God's covenant of shalom, the wholeness of supply!

God's covenant man (Gideon) faces off with the enemy and learns God's strategy for victory.

Verse thirty-four: God's covenant person is clothed with the Spirit of the Lord! God's dressing and preparation for battle is the armor of His Spirit (Ephesians 6:11-18). No Saul's armor for us, as David refused in his battle with Goliath!

We declare victory—blow a trumpet—before we see it! Just as the ancient shofars called from one shepherd to another, so our trumpeted declaration calls in others who are in agreement with God's purposes!

Verses thirty-six to forty, the matter of the fleece: God calls Gideon and us to a personal communion with Him, to be certain that this is God, not fleshly ambition or pride. Gideon uses the fleece as a means of ascertaining this. God knows his heart. It's not impertinence when you're God's covenant son or daughter!

Judges 7:1: Gideon and those with him camp beside a spring (Harod). In Hebrew, this is *En-Charod* (Strong's #5878), which means "a fountain of trembling." Gideon and his men know they are God's covenant people in the double portion. This makes them shake, overcome by God with them, in them. The word can imply fear, but here it is a healthy fear of the Lord when you know who He is and that He is for you!

God does a surprising thing in Judges 7:2-7. At least, He does a surprising thing in the natural but not in the spirit. He decreases Gideon's army. When we leave it to God, He does it! We submit to His plan and purposes, even when they seem contrary to what we think is common sense! Why did God do it this way?

1.   First, it protects those in fear. Some of Gideon's men were shaking with fear (v. 3). God knows that fear will open you up to the enemy and make you vulnerable, so He sets these ones aside for a time.

2.   Also, it keeps us in humility. God knows our flesh, that later we would try to take the credit and glory for ourselves. Once again, He saves us from ourselves in advance!

Principle: when God decreases you in some way as you're facing the enemy, praise Him! Because He is saving you from yourself and readying you for victory. It's a sign!

3.   Then, God eliminates those still trying to "do things the proper way." This is religion's way. The men in this passage who demonstrate this took their time preparing to drink. The others got about their drinking, hasting to be about God's victory. It is key that those men were ready to go now!

Judges 7:7 contains the declaration of victory in advance.

Principle: we get specific guidance and a guarantee of victory when we set our wills to choose God's way!

The men take what will strengthen their bodies and their spirits. The word "provisions" here in verse eight of Judges, chapter seven, in Hebrew is *tseydah* (Strong's #6720) and means "food" "meat." The word in the original language for trumpets is *shophar* (Strong's #7782), a ram's horn for declaring God's praise and goodness. It was clear sounding, like a cornet.

Gideon received a specific strategy as related in verse nine. In a dream or vision that night, the Lord God told Gideon, "Get up! Go down to their camp!" Notice the position of the Israelites was above their enemy, the Midianites, even in natural geography. They were above the enemy! Gideon must have thought he was hearing things because why would God tell him to go directly to the enemy's camp? It seemed contrary to logic, for sure! Yet Gideon believed and obeyed.

God also reveals that victory is sure (again!) and that Gideon is actually going to hear the plans of the enemy (vv. 9-11). The Lord even addresses fear in advance, and He tells Gideon he can take Purah, his servant, with him.

I believe God covered Gideon and his servant and made

them invisible to the enemy. How else were they able to creep into the camp's outskirts and overhear the Midianite man's dream? Notice in verses twelve to fourteen that Gideon and Purah not only hear the man's dream but its interpretation through his companion. God is so complete! We have all we need for the victory.

What was the purpose of Gideon hearing this since the dream appeared to have no specific strategy? It was so that he could be strengthened for victory (God declared this in verse eleven when He spoke to Gideon). The word "strengthened" here is *chazaq* (Strong's #2388), and we have seen it before; it means a fastening of all you are onto God! It is how David was able to recover all that was stolen from him at Ziklag as well as take the spoil of the enemy. I think of this word like a three-legged race, too: me attached to God now running the race!

Gideon's response to being so strengthened? *Worship* (v. 15)! He praises God.

Now he encourages the rest of the men.

Armed for battle (vv. 18-20): each man has a trumpet and an empty pitcher with a lamp inside. Hebrew here helps us understand more: "pitcher" is *kad* (Strong's # 3537), "an earthenware jar or pail." And "lamp" is *lappid* (Strong's #

3940), a "lamp," "flame," or "torch." The sound of God and His light in vessels of clay, like us. Amen!

Instructions for battle:

1. Blow the trumpets when Gideon does: "Do as I do" (Judges 7:17).

2. Declare whose side you are on: "For the Lord and for Gideon!" (Judges 7:18). This is a covenant!

Principle: the trumpets or shofars are a picture of the declaration. The shout is the agreement with God's declaration!

3. Smash the pitchers holding torches in their left hands and trumpets in their right. (Note there is no option of using their swords!)

4. Then they were to *shout*! And this is what they shouted, "The sword for the Lord and Gideon!" (Judges 7:20). Literally, *they* are God's sword against the enemy!

5. Finally, they were to *stand* (v. 21). And what happens? The enemy flees before them. Hebrew here is *amad* (Strong's # 5975): "stand," "abide." As in Ephesians 6:13-17 and Deuteronomy 28:7, having done all God has told you to do, you now stand and receive the victory. God does it! The enemy turns against itself and flees (v. 22).

God's strategy puts the enemy to flight through revelation gained by visitation to the enemy's camp. Victory is total! And God is still doing this today. Expect Him to speak and uncover the enemy's plan as well as encourage and strengthen you in the process. Hallelujah for the victory of the Lord!

Amen!

Strategy Eight

The Strategy of Humiliation

or Humility

2 Samuel 5-6

David

Humility: having an accurate estimation of yourself in Christ Jesus, who you are in the light of who He is and who you are in Him.

Humiliation: a process of getting you to the place of humility, usually through people or situations. Better to humble yourself (a choice) than to be humiliated, yet both arrive at the same place!

When the enemy comes up against you as God's covenant man or woman, this is a strategy that positions you for victory: *humility*! Again, you are operating in the opposite of the enemy. The devil knows pride and self-exaltation. The opposite, humility, undoes him and his purposes!

Here, in 2 Samuel, David has been made king over all Judah and Israel. He has known many victories in battle. In 2 Samuel, chapter five, we see King David has even just retaken Jerusalem. Yet, God is looking to move him into an even greater advantage over the enemy (2 Samuel 5:10).

The Key to His Victory (2 Samuel 5:12)

1. David perceived that the Lord had given him position and blessing, and all of it was for the purposes of God's kingdom. The word in Hebrew here for "perceived" is *yada* (Strong's #3045), meaning he "knew," "understood," "acknowledged," and "discerned."

2. Immediately, the anti-anointing comes after the anointing and the anointed one. In verse seventeen of chapter five, the Philistines come after King David and his kingdom.

What has been ruling is threatened by the anointing. This is a recognition in the spirit realm of good versus evil. It seeks to destroy the anointed one and the anointing. (Remember Herod and the infant Jesus!)

These Philistines come to the Valley of Rephaim, a valley of giants. Giants indicate an intermingling of evil with men.

3. The humble man, King David, gets even more humble (vv. 19-20). He acknowledges he doesn't know what to

do. How does he do this? He asks God what to do!

David refuses his instincts and impulses of the flesh. As he is a proven warrior, everything in him must have wanted to go to battle. But instead, he asks, "Shall I?"

He gets God's guarantee of victory. "Go, and I will deliver them into your hands" (2 Samuel 5:19, paraphrased). So, David goes against the Philistines in battle at Baal-Perazim. This is what David called it after God gave him victory there: he declared that God is the "Lord of breaking through" (2 Samuel 5:20). In Hebrew, the name of this city means "the possessor of the breaches," "the owner of the breaks" (Strong's #1188). Wow!

4. So David declares the Lord the owner of the breakthrough.

David himself is not the owner of the breaking through; it's God's!

David says God has given him victory as "the bursting out of great waters" (2 Samuel 5:20). The feeling in the Hebrew words, *perets* (Strong's #6556), meaning "bursting out," "breaking forth," and *mayim* (Strong's # 4325), meaning "flood," "spring" is of waters coming out of imprisonment or containment.

5. This will cause the enemy to lay down what he's been worshipping and the gods to which he's been paying

homage (v. 21). The Philistines here leave their idols right in the field of battle!

It's an acknowledgment by the enemy of who God is and how great is His power on behalf of those who are His.

Yet without your relationship with the Lord, a covenant relationship, the enemy will try again, even in the same place and same circumstance. In verse twenty-two, the Philistines once again come out to the Valley of Rephaim to battle David and Israel.

6. And again, David humbles himself and asks God in verse twenty-three if he should go out against them. God tells him *not* to go against the enemy directly. This appears contrary to what David would instinctively think to do and is the opposite of what God instructed before.

Principle: we must be willing to submit to God's plan and obey Him no matter how odd or unusual it may sound, and even though it isn't how we knew victory last time.

A familiar covenant relationship is *so* necessary to know and trust God this way. (Walking, talking with Him regularly!)

When we are set to obey, God will give a specific strategy (vv. 23-24). David was to wait for the sound of marching in the treetops and then advance. What caused this treetop marching? I think that would be angels! And their captain, the Lord!

God was saying, "Wait for the reserves!" The *maha-naim*, the two companies like those that Jacob saw. You go in with two companies, earthly and heavenly, and the enemy is routed once and for all. Amen!

Result: the enemy is consumed (v. 25).

7. The humiliation:
   a. Be careful to avoid presumption when you've exercised the strategy of humility and have known victory.
   b. The enemy is subtle, and pride can sneak up on you.
   c. Presumption: putting yourself in place of God. Your presumption hurts others. Dictionary definition of presumption: "the act of being so bold; taking for granted."[4]
   d. Here David, in chapter six of 2 Samuel, doesn't ask about moving the ark of the Lord (vv. 1-2). The ark of the covenant has been with Abinadab since the Philistines captured it and then returned it (1 Samuel 6).
   e. We can't presume we know how God's presence is going to move (or where and how and

by whom). David's heart was right to want to make a place for the presence of the Lord, but he needed to be in agreement with God's plan for this. That is what would protect him and the people.

f. You can't worship your own plan. In verse five, David and the people engaged in worship, but even if it looks like worship, God can't receive it if He isn't being lifted up and glorified.

g. In presumption, innocent people can die (v. 6). Wow!

We don't know everyone's covenant position in relation to God; they may be vulnerable to the evil one. Abinidab's son, Uzzah, one of those accompanying the cart carrying the ark, was killed instantly when he reached out a hand to steady the ark. We are shocked at this and think it is unfair, but God is God, and His glory is untouchable. David created this situation with his pride that paraded as a religious zeal.

8. Beware of displeasure and offense against God because He has had to humiliate you. Your own presumption, like David's, is what put you and others in this position. Here in verse eight, the word used is *charah* (Strong's # 2734), "to blaze up in anger, zeal, or jealousy," "be grieved," "fret self," "be incensed," "wroth."

David was mad at God! He was offended that God should act as He did!

Fear immediately follows the spirit of offense. David asks, "How then can the ark come to me?" (2 Samuel 6:9). "How can I know the presence of the Lord?"—this is what he should have asked first.

There was something not right in David's heart: What was his motivation for moving the ark? Remember, God looks at hearts! Abinadab had safely sheltered the ark, and now Obed-Edom (vv. 10-11) did: men of humility and simple hearts.

9.   David examines his heart.

Humiliation should drive us here. We need to get past offense and fear and view our hearts with the Holy Spirit. David backs off and submits to God's immediate plan for the ark to remain with Obed-Edom. And did God work in and transform David's heart in these three months? I'm sure He did! Now David is ready for God's plan.

David sees that blessing accompanies the ark. God's presence is its own reward (vv. 11-12). I believe David's heart exam led him to desire the ark for the right reasons: not just for himself and a symbol of his kingship, but for *all* the people.

He brought the ark up with gladness! *Simchah* (Strong's #8057): "glee," "joyfulness," "rejoicing."

Notice too, the ark of the covenant had to be carried by men, not transported on a cart! It's a symbol of God's presence occupying our humble vessels of flesh.

It must be God's plan and God's way with the fear, reverence, worship of the Lord! God is El Olam, the everlasting God who will be what He will be! We don't know all His ways, but we can seek and agree with them.

David tried the first time to move the ark in the world's way (1 Samuel 6:7-8; how the Philistines sent it back after having captured it). Now, he moves it in God's way, carried by Aaron's descendants, the Levites (1 Chronicles 15:1-16, 26-29; 16:1), and accompanied by sacrifices and worship.

10. Blessing comes to the many when we agree with and walk in God's way (2 Samuel 6:15, 18, 19):
   a. Spiritual blessing: joy in worship and God's presence corporately;
   b. Physical blessing: material evidence; here, all the people got bread, meat, and raisin cakes to take home.

David's own household gets blessed (v. 20).

11. The religious spirit (the seed of the old thing: here,

Saul's daughter, Michal) will condemn your newfound joy and freedom in the Lord, and its pathway, humility, and humiliation (v. 20). This spirit despises worship, that is, true worship! When adultery with the world's ways was evidenced in Saul, he lost the true anointing and became the vehicle for the anti-anointing.

12. There is a declaration of joy in true humility, a true knowledge of the Lord and who you are in Him (vv. 21-22).

Those in the agreement will see and rejoice. Those against the true anointing of God will know barrenness. That is, they will have no fruit that survives (v. 23). Here we see this in 2 Samuel 6:23 in Michal, Saul's daughter, who mocked King David and his unrestrained worship.

After this outbreak of joy, rest results! In Samuel 7:1, we see that this was true for David and the Israelites. Hostilities with the enemy ceased.

Hallelujah! As we submit to the strategy of humility, and yes, even humiliation (King David did both!), God can position us for blessing and rest. And yes, this extends to our households and those who surround us as well. Go down so you can be lifted up to His high places, and the enemy will flee from you and all surrounding you. Amen!

"The Water Song" from *Hind's Feet on High Places* by Hannah Hurnard

Come, oh come! let us away—

Lower, lower every day,

Oh, what joy it is to race

Down to find the lowest place.

This is the dearest law we know—

"It is happy to go low."

Sweetest urge and sweetest will,

"Let us go down lower still."

Hear the summons night and day

Calling us to come away.

From the heights we leap and flow

To the valleys down below.

Always answering to the call,

To the lowest place of all.

Sweetest urge and sweetest pain,

To go low and rise again.[5]

Strategy Nine.

The Strategy of Love

Genesis 39, 42–45; 1 Corinthians 13:4-8

Joseph

When confronted by our enemy, Satan, face-to-face, God's strategy of love will deliver you and put him to flight! Satan knows nothing of love; he has no basis in his nature for love. He rejected God, and God *is* love. Indeed, envy and jealousy, the perversion of love, caused his fall from heaven. Calvary love, the love that moved God to come in the form of man to bridge the gap between Himself and us, totally caught the devil off guard. He was defeated because love was so much higher than him and his nature, so much that he couldn't retaliate against that thing he couldn't understand and see.

1.   When in face-to-face battle with the enemy, if we choose to love, we will know victory (Matthew 5:44-45).

  a.   Love protects you!

  b.   Love opens the door to redemption for the one

the enemy is using (Proverbs 25:21-22).

2.   Stay in the love of the Lord no matter what! "Love endures long and is patient and kind…" (1 Corinthians 13:4a).

   a.   Joseph endured twenty-two years and stayed in God's love for his brothers, who did him wrong. How do we know?

   - He was able to move forward with the Lord, even in what appeared like captivity!

   - He had peace, so circumstances and people didn't move him.

   - He was prepared when his "enemies" (those who had done him wrong) came to the place where God could work.

   b.   Joseph was patient for God to do the victory and restoration His way. Even when reunited with his brothers, Joseph didn't rush to restore his own way or present his own case or defend himself.

Principle: those who operate in love have received God's love! First Corinthians 13:4b says love is never jealous or envious.

3. Jealousy is the perversion of love. It operates when one has no true understanding of being loved by the Father God. This invites comparison.

The one operating in jealousy receives condemnation.

Jealousy feels it must lay hold of its own inheritance. There is no security that love (that is *love*, the Father God) will provide.

4. Joseph knew his father's love and His Father's love! He understood the covenant under which he stood as a son. Firstly, Joseph understood it in the natural (Genesis 37:3). Secondly, and most importantly, he knew the truth in the spiritual. "The Lord was with Joseph," the Scripture says over and over (Genesis 39:2, 3, 5, 21, 23). Genesis 41:38 states that it was evident that God's spirit was in Joseph. He bore his Father's likeness. There was a family resemblance!

Because Joseph knew that he was loved, the hatred and jealousy of his enemies could *not* move him. He knew his covenant inheritance in his Father God, and so, in the face of hate, jealousy, and manipulation, he loved.

5. The humility of love will protect you! First Corinthians 13:4b continues, "[love] is not boastful or vainglorious."

The enemy is counting on you to defend yourself by counting up your own righteousness. Thereby he can exploit your flesh.

When you refuse to do this and say, "It is *all* God," then you undo the enemy! He cannot work with humility, as we learned in the previous chapter. Humility indicates proper order and position through Christ in God. The enemy is kicked out in such a situation. Amen!

Joseph knew his Father had preserved, delivered, protected, and advanced him. Everything was God (Genesis 41:16, 51-52; 45:5-9).

Such love then prepares the way of blessing for even those who were against you; that is, Joseph, as a leader in Egypt, provided in advance for his own brothers and all his family.

"Love is not vain, is not puffed up" (1 Corinthians 13:5a, Interlinear Bible). In the original Greek of this verse, the word is *perpereuomai* (Strong's #4068), which means to "vaunt itself." Another similar word in Greek is *phusioo* (Strong's #5448), which means "to inflate itself." Again, in the face of the enemy, you don't have to make yourself seem bigger for him to flee. You look *big* in the spirit! He will flee when he sees Jesus in you! We're not like those animals in the wild that must use adaptations to appear larger. The Lord is Who fights for you! When you act like

He acts, submitted to the Father, and then you give God all the glory, the enemy of your soul sees God and not you. And the devil *will* flee! Resist coming into agreement with the devil and his ways. Agree with God, and His *charakter* (His Spirit evidenced) in you will put the enemy to flight. Amen!

6.   Principle: you can't win God's victory with the enemy's tactics (1 Corinthians 13:5b).

    a.   Resist rudeness, i.e., hurtful remarks and attacks. Don't fight flesh with the flesh; overcome evil with good—the spirit of love (Romans 12:21). In the Amplified Bible, Classic Edition, version of 1 Corinthians 13:5b, it says love does not act "unbecomingly." In other words, don't act as if you belong to the father of this world, the devil!

    b.   Give up the right to be right! This doesn't mean you aren't right or on the side of what is right, but lay down your fleshly, natural right to be justified and allow God to justify and defend you.

    c.   Give up the right to be offended! Once again, 1 Corinthians 13:5b says, "[love] is not touchy or fretful or resentful…" The enemy will try to stir up your flesh, but James 4:4-7 reminds us that as we resist this agreement in our flesh, he *must* flee. *Victory!*

d. Give up the rehearsal of offenses against you since love "thinketh no evil" (1 Corinthians 13:5, KJV). This means in your mind and on your lips (Proverbs 23:7a). Keep your confession in line with God's Word, and you will see the fruit of your lips created (Proverbs 18:20-21).

Joseph didn't fight flesh with the flesh. What had been done to him was evil, but he refused evil and kept himself in agreement with God's covenant and God's desire for covenant in others. He wasn't unbecoming God's covenant person, but rather, he became more like God. He extended grace, received God's strategies (fighting in the flesh will block these!), and gave up his rights to dwell on the offenses and the offenders.

Key: as a result, God honored Joseph with victory and restoration!

7. Stay in the truth, and the truth will defend and free you (1 Corinthians 13:6). Love majors in the truth!

We say, "Whose side is God on?" His question: "Who is on *My* side?" The truth's side, that is! John 14:6 tells us that He is truth. Stay on God's side, and He says, "If I am for you, who can be against you?" (Romans 8:31, paraphrased).

8. Choose to have God's heart for your enemy.

This can only come from the love you receive from your heavenly Father that positions you as a son or daughter of His. There is no successful threat when you know who you are and whose you are.

Having received grace and love, you can extend it! Joseph's desire for his brothers was restoration with himself and God and the multiplication and extension of the covenant blessing to them. First Corinthians 13:7 (paraphrased) says:

"Love bears all things…" It isn't overcome by evil!

"Love believes all things…" Faith isn't affected; it is not moved.

"Love endures all things…" It doesn't receive what is not of God's covenant, so it can't change your position. Patience is possible.

Principle: faith + patience = desired outcome (Hebrews 10:36).

9. Love will always win!

10. Victory is sure if you will love in the face of dark-

ness and evil (1 John 4:18; 5:1-5).

Faith is the victory!

Hope is the victory!

Love is the victory!

Love will break witchcraft and evil—you can't be controlled if you don't submit to it—and will guarantee the full purposes of God in you and others!

"Love never fails..." (1 Corinthians 13:8).

Amen!

Strategy Ten.

The Strategy of Anointed Single-Mindedness

Caleb

Single-mindedness: having only one purpose in mind; sincere, straightforward; single-hearted.

Anointed single-mindedness: unwavering agreement with God's purpose, mind, heart, and will.

Scripture references for this teaching: Numbers 13:17-33; 14:6-10, 24; Joshua 14:6-14, 15:13-19; James 1:6-8; Isaiah 50:7.

When you face the enemy, the strategy of anointed single-mindedness will deliver you into the fullness of God's promised inheritance for you and your seed.

Single-mindedness sees with God's eyes.

1. The appearance of things in the natural doesn't de-

ter sight with the prophetic eye. In Numbers 13:22, Caleb, one of those chosen by the Israelites to spy out the promised land, Canaan, disregarded as inconsequential to God's purpose three giants and their strongholds in the land.

2. Single-mindedness gathers fruit in the presence of the enemy (Numbers 13:23, 24). Also, there is a reference in Psalm 23:5 where the psalmist tells us the Lord prepares a table for us in the presence of our enemies. This fruit is evidence of the promise!

3. The fruit must be sought to be gathered! Note: all this is previctory! The enemy is still encamped against you.

4. Double-mindedness (here, personified by the ten spies other than Caleb and Joshua) disregards the fruit and its promise and focuses on the circumstances and apparent strength of the enemy (Numbers 13:27-29).

Single-mindedness declares God's purpose and victory *before* it is accomplished and *in spite of* the occupation of the enemy (v. 30).

Double-mindedness sees itself through the eyes of the enemy rather than in the light of *Who* the Lord God is! That is, the single-minded man or woman sees himself or herself the way God does and the way His Word declares (v. 33).

Principle: a double-minded person is undecided in mind and wavers. That person is "up for grabs" to the enemy.

The single-minded man or woman is the Lord's!

Rather than the prophetic word determining who that person is, the double-minded one receives and declares over himself or herself the report of the enemy.

The single-minded person goes forward without the agreement of most others, as long as that one is certain of the agreement of the Lord with his or her purpose (Numbers 14:1-6).

1.   Single-mindedness travails for those in fear who would turn back. *Such ones always have the heart of the Lord for others!*

2.   That one keeps speaking the Word: God is good, and His inheritance, which He has led us to, is good. No matter how it seems (Numbers 14:7, 8). Scripture describes it as "a land flowing with milk and honey" (Exodus 3:17); the best of all possible provision is understood in this phrase.

3.   Single-mindedness speaks against fear and rebellion (v. 9).

4.   Single-mindedness declares its covenant with almighty God: "The Lord is with us!" Joshua and Caleb say so in verse nine; also, Romans 8:31 goes even further when it says, "If God is for us, who can be against us?" (my paraphrase).

5.   Don't be surprised when those who are wavering and double-minded want to kill you and the anointing of God in you (v. 10).

6.   God's *glory* (Hebrew *kabod*) will defend you (v. 10). *All He is*, the weight of all His goodness, will preserve and protect and keep you. The Hebrew word *kabod* (Strong's #3519) means "weight," "splendor," "copiousness." The related word *kabad* (Strong's #3513) means "heaviness," "abounding with," "be glorious," "great." The Word says you carry His glory within you. Wear it, and the enemy will flee!

Single-mindedness intercedes for those in opposition, even those threatening death, and pleads for their inheritance for God's name's sake (Numbers 14:11-20). Moses does this here, and God pardons these ones in response.

Such a one asks for mercy and grace for the offender.

The Lord will agree to preserve the offenders' lives, but their inheritance may not manifest here on the earth because of their unbelief (vv. 22-23).

The single-minded one (here, Caleb in verse twenty-four) is promised victory and fullness of the manifestation of his or her inheritance here on the earth. In this verse, the word "wholeheartedly" in Hebrew is *male* (Strong's #4392), which means "fullness," "filled with." It is from another *male* (Strong's #4390), which means "to fill or be full of," "have wholly." In the strategy of single-mindedness, you, like Caleb, are so full of God and His Word that the enemy can't get a false word or circumstance in edgewise. Amen!

This is to you *and* your seed. In verse twenty-four, it says that Caleb (you) will live in the land and that his seed shall possess it. Amen!

Principle: God's promises always go beyond you to your seed. He sees them as one and the same for blessing purposes.

After the battles to possess the land (and there *will* be battles, but you *will* come through them), the single-minded man or woman reminds God of His promises (Joshua 14:6-10) and of his or her agreement with them right in the enemy's face. God loves this (Isaiah 62:6-12). Wow! In covenant privilege, we see the relationship as Daddy/daughter, Daddy/son, and Husband/wife.

Single-mindedness declares the Word as strongly today as when it first received the Word of the Lord and went into battle (Joshua 14:11; Deuteronomy 28:6). Coming in and going out...The word "strength" here in verse eleven of Joshua, chapter fourteen, is *kowach* in Hebrew (Strong's

#3581), meaning "firmness," "vigor," "force." See also Psalm 92:12-15.

Caleb declares that his mind has not changed or moved from the purposes of the Lord, and this has made him strong and given him the power to overcome. Amen! (See Isaiah 26:3; Romans 8:5-6; Philippians 1:27-28.)

The single-minded man or woman claims his or her covenant portion boldly (Joshua 14:12).

Such a one has no fear over the currently occupying enemy (Proverbs 13:22; Deuteronomy 8:18).

Those in the anointing and truth will bless you and agree (v. 13). Joshua blesses Caleb and gives him the land of Hebron as his inheritance as promised.

Your seed will know and claim the double portion (Joshua 15:13-19).

1. You will have driven out the giants before them (v. 14). Caleb did this!

2. You will have seen *godly* life overcome carnal knowledge and works (vv. 15-17). What is God trumps what looks apparent in the flesh.

3. Your seed will be married to the Lion of God, Jesus. (Caleb's daughter, Achsah, married Othniel, whose

name means "lion of El, or God"[6]). They will be wed together in covenant life!

4. Your seed has her Bridegroom's consent to ask for her inheritance and receive *boldly*, even *double*. Othniel gave Achsah consent to ask her father for her portion, and he gave her not just the land with springs she requested but land with upper and lower springs.

Double-mindedness (wavering between two minds: the mind of Christ, lined up with the Word, versus the mind of the flesh, lined up with the natural) will rob you of your covenant portion and victory.

No agreement with the Word = no fruit!

Principle: faith and fear *cannot* occupy the same space. "You cannot serve God and mammon..." (Matthew 6:24). "Mammon" here in Greek is *mammonas* (Strong's #3126), meaning "confidence," i.e. "figuratively, wealth personified," "greed." In other words, you cannot serve God at the same time as you serve what there is in the natural that supports you or makes you confident.

Single-mindedness preserves the victory (Isaiah 50:7).

The Lord has my eyes and my ears; the gates are only open to Him! Thus, every gate of the enemy is taken (Genesis 22:17; Isaiah 50:4-6).

No shame! What God has promised *must and will* come to pass!

Praise God that the enemy is put to flight by our single-minded agreement with our covenant God through Jesus Christ, His Son!

Amen!

Strategy Eleven.

The Strategy of Thankfulness/Thanksgiving

Daniel

Now when Daniel knew that the writing was signed, he went into his house, and his windows being opened in his chamber toward Jerusalem, he got down upon his knees three times a day and prayed and gave thanks before his God as he had done previously.

Daniel 6:10

Thankfulness: the act of feeling or expressing thanks; being grateful (full of gratitude).

Thanksgiving: the giving of thanks, especially to God.

When the enemy faces off with you, the strategy of thankfulness will cut him off and put him to flight. Amen!

1. The favor of the Lord, in His covenant with you, will bring you advancement and honor even in prison or any type of captivity (Daniel 1:9, 17, 20).

    a. Daniel had a revelation (from God!), wisdom, and knowledge in advance of a thing (Daniel 2:16-24).

    b. Such revelation provided deliverance for many.

    c. Daniel gave glory to God for the gift of revelation (Daniel 2:28, 47-49).

    d. The result was honor to God's man or woman used by God to reveal the truth (Daniel 5:29; 6:2-3).

2. This honor God gives you, and the excellent spirit of the Lord observed in you will stir up the enemy against you.

"An excellent spirit" was said to be in Daniel (Daniel 6:3, KJV). The word used here in Hebrew is *yattiyr* (Strong's #3493), which means "preeminent," "exceedingly." This correlates to *yathiyr* or *jattir* (Strong's #3492), which means "redundant," derived from *yathar* (Strong's #3498), meaning "to jut over or exceed," "cause to abound," "preserve."

In other words, the head and *not* the tail (Deuteronomy 28:13) in *everything*, and redundantly so. Amen!

This is what a covenant relationship with God positions you for and produces in you! The spirit of excellence is a characteristic of God's man or woman, and its opposite in our enemy, the devil, is a foul and unclean spirit.

The foul and unclean spirit joins with a spirit of jealousy and accusation to attack and destroy you. This is what was happening with Daniel in Daniel, chapter six. Such a spirit is a warring spirit and moves against God and His own.

Whenever the prosperity of God abounds, the enemy will attack and try to get you to *move* (Genesis 26:12-16).

In that scripture, Isaac moved, but in Christ, you *stand*. This is the new covenant! The enemy moves and flees as you stand on the Word (Ephesians 6:11, 13-14). Four times in these verses, it declares that we *stand*. The word in Greek is *histemi* (Strong's #2476) and means "abide," "continue," "hold up." These are our new marching orders in Christ Jesus! In Acts 17:28 and 20:24, we learn what moves us: the living Word in us only, *not* the enemy! We make him move, flee! So, *stay* in the Word!

Here in Daniel 6:4-5, the attack comes from Daniel's peers and seeming friends, even the ones he had previously saved by his interpretation of a dream (Daniel 2:24).

You should be prepared for the attack to be undeserved by you. It is not just; the enemy never is!

Principle: don't look for justice but never fail to extend it.

Resolve to not stay in grief too long over an instrument of jealousy, accusation, and witchcraft. If you stay in your grief, it will affect your ability to stay in thankfulness.

The enemy uses flattery; that is, he taps into the flesh and pride of those in position against you (Daniel 6:6-9).

3. Immediately, as God reveals to you the intent (the words, the legal intention) of the enemy, you give thanks (Daniel 6:10).

    a. Note: Daniel had a habit of giving thanks. In Daniel 6:10, it says, "…as he had done previously."

We need to be staying in a customary attitude of thankfulness so that when the plan of the enemy is released against us, we immediately know what to do. Scripture says Daniel prayed three times a day: morning, noon, and night. In other words, his prayer life was constant.

    b. Play the "thankful game"! Find all the things you have for which to be thankful. See Psalms 30:4; 105:1; Ephesians 5:20; Colossians 3:17; 1

Thessalonians 5:18.

   c. Immediately, when you thank God for one blessing, the way is made for the double to come in. God's will *is* always double, multiplied, *more*.

4. The moment Daniel gave thanks, he was positioned for deliverance, and the mouths of the lions (and his accusers!) were shut and unable to do Daniel harm.

Even though it appears otherwise, don't let that move you! Daniel believed God had heard him and received his thanks and so had guaranteed his victory, even though he still was put in the den of the lions.

Principle: covenant love and position are higher than the law of man. It appears the law must be fulfilled as here, where Daniel must serve the penalty the law required for those making petition to anyone other than the king, but God's covenant promises abound over legality (Daniel 6:11-16).

5. What do we give thanks for in such a situation? What did Daniel thank God for?

   a. For Who God is and how He has revealed Himself to us by His wondrous names. Worship! See "The Thankful Song" in 1 Chronicles 16:7-36, 41.

  b. For the outcome being declared in advance. Romans 4:17 says that God calls things that are not as though they already were, and so should we. Agree with God!

He watches over His word to perform it, as Jeremiah 1:12 says. Thank Him for that; it's not up to you.

As you thank God in this way and acknowledge Him as being in control and the source of all that is good for you, you bring kingdom order to the situation. Genesis 1:26-28 reveals God's original plan, and it hasn't changed:

- dominion over all created things, including Satan, a fallen angel;

- fruitfulness: blessing;

- multiplication: the redundantly abundant.

We do *not* give thanks for the evil, but we rejoice in thankfulness that even the evil becomes an instrument of God's good to and for us (Romans 8:28; Genesis 50:20). Never thank God for evil itself but for how it serves God and His glorious purposes.

  6. Giving thanks, being full of thankfulness, brings in the angels to serve with you (Daniel 6:22). *Mahanaim!* As we learned before with Jacob, we now become two companies: ourselves and the angels with us. Here, the angel God

sent for Daniel actually shut the lions' mouths.

7. No hurt of any kind can come to you if you stay in the strategy of thankfulness (Daniel 6:23; Luke 10:19-20). The word for "harm" here in Daniel is *chabal* (Strong's #2257), which means "harm," "damage," "hurt," derived from *chabal* (Strong's #2255), which means "to ruin," "destroy." These correspond to *chabal* (Strong's #2254): "to wind tightly as a rope," "to bind," "pervert," "destroy," "withhold," "writhe in pain."

In other words, nothing the devil intends can touch you and what concerns you. He doesn't "bind" you; you bind him!

    a. Even here, in the Luke scripture, the Lord says, "Don't rejoice or major in your authority over the enemy but remember you only have it because it's Mine, and I save you from yourself too!" Again, a position of humility. The enemy must flee!

    b. The enemy is totally consumed. God defends you! In verse twenty-four of Daniel, chapter six, those who had accused Daniel met the fate planned for him.

Thus, the outcome for ones who are instruments of evil may grieve you, but it is necessary—the wages of sin without the covering of the Blood!

8.   God gets *all* the glory (Daniel 6:25-27). Men praise Him and declare who He is. Here, King Darius is now talking God's order!

Those in authority become instruments of God's righteousness. God's kingdom advances—even in the midst of worldliness—here, personified by Babylon.

God's people/person (Daniel, you, and I) will prosper. In verse twenty-eight, the Hebrew word is *tselach* (Strong's #6744), meaning "advance," "prosper," and is related to *tsaleach* (Strong's #6743), a root word meaning, "to push forward," "break out," "come mightily," go over." Wow!

This is God's plan for us as we utilize the strategy of thankfulness. Let your thankful heart bring the enemy to his knees as you then go forward as God's kingdom does the same—to be redundantly abundant!

Amen!

Strategy Twelve.

The Strategy of the Table

Psalm Twenty-Three

When the enemy threatens you and is in your face attempting to kill or destroy you and steal from you and your seed, seek the Lord at His table.

The Principle of Passover

1. When the enemy was coming against Israel, the Lord called them to His table.

Their enemies threatened Israel's liberty and the fullness of covenant life (Exodus 13:9-10; 14:1-14).

2. In the natural, it looked like the pharaoh and Egypt would keep Israel from leaving, yet God's Passover, the symbol of His covenant, declared them free *before* they actually were.

3. This is a picture of Jesus's death and resurrection and the establishment of the new covenant.

Jesus's Example (1 Corinthians 11:23-30)

1. Jesus called His disciples to the table while the betrayal against Him was in progress.

2. Meeting at the table involves thankfulness, our last strategy. Here in verse twenty-four, Paul recounts how Jesus gave thanks first.

3. This meal Jesus had with His disciples declared that the Father would be mindful of His covenant with His Son, and so we declare, with us, through Him (vv. 24-25).

4. Partaking of His body, blood, death, and resurrection through this remembrance via the elements of the table declares that you are an heir to that new covenant inheritance. Amen!

5. We are cautioned not to eat or drink unworthily at His table (vv. 27-28). Here the word in the original Greek is *anaxios* (Strong's #371), which means "irreverently." It's from *anaxios* (Strong's #370), meaning "unfit," "not deserving, comparable, or suitable." In other words, don't come to the Lord's table if you don't know who you are in Him and that you belong there. You can't come like a visitor; it's for family. Hallelujah!

Verse thirty explains why there are many not whole or

even those who die prematurely. It's because they don't come to the table of the Lord as covenant people, having examined themselves by the Holy Spirit within them.

God's Purpose for His Table

1. This is a declaration of your covenant with Him and of His with you through Jesus Christ, your Savior, done in the very presence of your enemies (Psalm 23:5).

2. He has prepared this table for you. He has made it ready, completed it. In Psalm 23:5, the Hebrew word for "prepare" is *arak* (Strong's #6186), which means "arranged," "put in order," "joined the battle," "expert in war," ordained." See Colossians 2:14-15. Wow!

3. Our response to this preparation? To come and dine, to partake of what He has won and prepared for us. Amen!

I like to think of this as when I sat at the table as a child in my parents' home. If the phone rang or someone came to the door for me, my parents would say, "She can't come; she's at the table, sitting down to eat." I like to think God tells Satan when he beckons war, "Debbie's at My table. You aren't allowed to bother her!"

So, what's for dinner at God's table? What does the enemy see when he views me there?

1. He sees the Lord our Shepherd, Jehovah Raah/Raphah. The devil observes that you are sitting at *the Lord's* table, that He Himself is there with you. The evil one sees the *good* Shepherd, the Shepherd of *all* that is good, and you are partaking of that good. The Hebrew word *raah* (Strong's #7462) is "to tend a flock," "to pasture it," "to rule," "to associate with as a friend."

Principle: when the enemy sees me at the table of the Lord, he perceives that the Lord has called me His friend. See John 15:11-15; Genesis 18:17; Isaiah 41:8; James 2:23. *Wow!*

2. Because you participate at the table of the Lord as an invited friend, a covenant person, you declare your portion and inheritance is to lack nothing. Nothing missing, nothing broken—the very definition of *shalom* (2 Peter 1:2-4).

By the same token, as you sit down at the table with your very good Friend, your Shepherd Jesus, the act of eating and drinking there declares that anything that is *not* good is *not* your portion. You refuse what the devil's handing out and attempting to bring against you.

3. There's *rest* at the table in the midst of war (Psalm

23:2).

Rest = food = sustenance; rest = drink = peace. The eating (pastures), that is, the bread of the Word, and partaking of the cup that represents His Blood shed for us to seal our covenant bless us *so that we can declare rest before we see rest.*

Principle: having been so declared, rest must come.

4.   There's restoration here for your soul (Psalm 23:3). The word in Hebrew for "restore" is *shuwb* (Strong's #7725), meaning "return to its starting point or home." So here at the table, the Lord returns my soul (my mind, my will, and my emotions) to their starting point, to retreat in the most refreshing sense of that word, to Him! To the ultimate place of rest and wholeness: God and His Word.

Any soulish or fleshly thoughts, emotions, and impulses of your will He pulls into line with Himself as you partake at His table. These very soul snares/traps are what would give the enemy advantage and opportunity over you.

He reminds us that we have His righteousness in us. His right ways of doing and being, as we agree with Him, are now imparted into us through Him, the Lord of righteousness. So, we can expect right and good will come forth from us as well.

The enemy is directed to look at God, not us. In verse

three of psalm twenty-three, it says, "for His name's sake." The enemy sees our covenant partner, Jesus, as we are covered at the table.

5. There's victory at the table over *all* the fruit of death (Psalm 23:4).

Allow no fear, and evil will flee. Why? Because the Lord is with us!

The Lord's rod and staff comfort us. Years ago, I heard Allegra McBirney speaking at a Christian women's conference at America's Keswick in New Jersey call these "the perfect pair for perfect care." The Hebrew word for "rod" is *shebet* (Strong's #7626), "a scepter," "staff," "rod or stick of correction." "Staff" is *mishteneth* (Strong's #4938), meaning "support," "a sustenance," "walking stick." And the word "comfort" is *nacham* (Strong's # 5162), declaring "sigh," i.e., "breathe strongly," "console," "comfort." The enemy and his weapon of death, and even the threat of death, can't touch me because I am in covenant with the Lord, and His rod and staff, His very Word and life, give me access to all that is His (like when the king extended his scepter to Esther). He corrects me when I need to get back on track and supports me as I walk this life. Amen! The devil doesn't correct me or have anything to do with me. I am not his; *I am the Lord's*!

Many years ago, in a vision, the Lord showed me that only *He* weeds His garden—*me* in Him. He has called me His garden, as in Song of Solomon, and He delights to walk with me there, as He tends to anything in my life that is not of Him, and He uproots it.

Principle: the privilege of the covenant relationship shuts all others out.

6.   The overflow of the anointing is at the table (Psalm 23:5). I'm not just full; I'm full to overflowing.

The enemy can't see me for the anointing on me. He only sees the fullness of the Anointed One, Jesus, and His anointing, so he flees (Psalms 20:6; 28:8; 105:15). I am smeared with the anointing, the fatness of the Anointed One and His anointing, and it keeps the enemy from touching me (I'm slippery!) and from seeing clearly (I'm smeared!) the victory that is sure to come. The Lord told me this kept the devil from seeing the victory of Jesus's resurrection as well. Wow!

The Strategy of the Table thwarts the enemy as it and what it represents declare that I am in covenant inheritance with the Lord Jesus Christ (Psalm 23:6). As such, I will receive only:

1.   goodness (Hebrew *towb* [Strong's #2896], "good"

in the widest sense);

2. mercy (Hebrew *checed* [Strong's #2617], "kind-ness");

3. The love of God forever! Unfailing love! The actual meaning of *checed* implies "loving-kindness"; you can't separate the two. His love will always extend His kindness to me.

As I come to the table, I declare that the Lord is my dwelling place, my place to abide forever. *I live in all that He is.* Hallelujah!

Take Communion now and come to His table, reflecting on all we have just declared. Claim the victory here!

A Quick Review and Guide

Satan's Strategies against God's Covenant People

Capture the flag: territory war, compromise

Blitz attack: many fronts

Blame game: accusation

Hide and seek

Sympathy for the enemy

God's Strategies for Overcoming and Victory

The Strategy of Praise: Jehoshaphat

The Strategy of Prayer: Abraham

The Strategy of Obedience: Moses

The Strategy of Standing: David

The Strategy of Wrestling before God: Jacob

The Strategy of Purity: Job (Character)

The Strategy of Entering the Enemy's Camp: Gideon

The Strategy of Humiliation or Humility: David

The Strategy of Love: Joseph

The Strategy of Anointed Single-Mindedness: Caleb

The Strategy of Thankfulness/Thanksgiving: Daniel

The Strategy of the Table: Psalm Twenty-Three

Epilogue

I pray that the lives of these Biblical examples have encouraged your heart to expect to overcome daily. Some might look at these as only old covenant examples with nothing to say to us as we are in Christ under the new covenant. But as the Scriptures plainly show, God's plan runs from Genesis through Revelation consistently. Jesus came to fulfill the Law and to restore us to God Himself so that by faith in Jesus, we might be restored to the plan that God intended for humanity from the very beginning in the Garden of Eden. What a perfect plan! What a wonderful, loving, restoring God!

Notes

Endnotes

1   James Strong, *The New Strong's Exhaustive Concordance of the Bible* (Nashville, TN: Thomas Nelson Publishers, 1990). Hereinafter abbreviated as Strong's.

2   *Webster's New World Dictionary for Young Readers*, David B. Guralnik, editor in chief s.v. "praise" (New York, NY: Simon and Schuster, Inc., 1983), 573.

3   William Smith, Jr., *Smith's Bible Dictionary* (Uhrichsville, OH: Barbour and Company, 1987), 37.

4   *Webster's New World Dictionary for Young Readers*, David B. Guralnik, editor in chief s.v. "presumption" (New York, NY: Simon and Schuster, Inc., 1983), 578.

5   Hannah Hurnard, *Hinds Feet on High Places* (Blacksburg, VA: Wilder Publications, 2010), 28.

6   William Smith, Jr., *Smith's Bible Dictionary* (Uhrichsville, OH: Barbour and Company, 1987), 228.

9 781685 561093